For Magdalena

Getting Ready *to* MOVE OUT

A Guidebook

to Help Young Adults Prepare for Moving Out

Thanks for your support

Ashley

ASHLEY ANELLO

First Edition

PAGE PUBLISHING, INC.
New York, NY

First originally published by Page Publishing, Inc. 2018

ISBN 978-1-64298-191-9 (Paperback)
ISBN 978-1-64298-189-6 (Digital)

Printed in the United States of America

To Tamara Stark, thank you for your support while I worked on this project that will help prepare young people to go out and join the world of adult responsibility and work for the rest of their lives because they have no idea how good they have it at home.

To Jen Anello, my daughter, to whom I will gift the first copy for Mikayla K. Corn, my granddaughter. I am very proud of both of you and the hard work you do to have better futures for yourselves.

To Joe Anello II, my son, who will receive the second copy for Jia E. Anello-Cho, my granddaughter. I am very proud of you and the man you have become.

I love all of you, forever.

Introduction

Now that you have finished high school or college and can't wait to start your new life without rules and curfews, let's check out how you can do it.

This is for *all* young people who have lived with parents or providers from birth until today. Now is the time that you have chosen (or have been asked) to forge out on your own and create a life on your own terms. If you are not headed to a dormitory at some college or live at home while finishing college and if you're eighteen, you may need to read this to help you decide if you really can afford to say goodbye to your parents or guardians, move out of their house, and start your Sunday dinner visits, holiday visits, and occasional visits to do your laundry.

Are you ready to be a grown-up and start taking the adult financial responsibilities that go along with this life-changing step? Before you decide to do this, start at the beginning of this book, read it over, think about what you read, and do the math as you go along.

If you are in a foster care program and will age out soon, this is the time to start getting yourself ready for living on your own. As a young adult aging out of a foster program, you have no fallback parents and may not have anyone able support to you. You have to get it right when you walk out that door. I recommend you review the Resources section for guidance.

Here are a few things you need to know in order to survive the move out and how to keep ahead of the game of life as an adult.

Most of these things will fall in the same order of importance, and they will all happen at the same time or so close together that it will feel that way. Most adults feel overwhelmed every day by the way all this stuff goes on simultaneously.

Adults know how this feels and will be able to relate because of their personal experience. Some of you will take adult advice, most of you will not.

You don't have a choice when it comes to becoming an adult. The tough part of this time in your life is how and who helped you get this far, if you even had help at all. No child is born with a guide book, and not everyone makes good decisions and choices when it comes to pregnancy and having children. Not everyone is blessed with wonderful, loving, caring and nurturing parents either. Lots of young adults were raised in homes by adults that had very little or no skills at all in the arena of parenting. Some were raised by alcoholics, drug abusers, homes with abusive parents, domestic violence and many are sexually abused at home.

Parents and guardians do the best they can with what they know. Many walk away and give their children up for adoption because they think their children deserve a better life than the biological parent can give them, and lots of children end up in foster programs.

There are lots of good foster families, and there are lots of bad foster families. Being in a foster program is very difficult emotionally and can be limiting. Some kids and young adults live in fear of rejection, abuse, criticism and many other things that can scar them for life, others have a better experience and are placed in good homes with; families that really care to make a difference. If you are leaving home or a foster program, once out there in the world, the rules are the same. You are on your own, the only difference is one group of young adults has fall back parents and another has no fall back parents. The bottom line for all kinds of young adults is that when you are 18 and move out, it is your turn to be in charge of your life. Your decisions, choices and actions are what will make you the real person you will be as an adult. At 18, you know right from wrong, and hopefully you will always strive to make the right choices.

If you are one of the young adults that came from a bad situation, the memory may not go away, but the future that you have ahead of you is what you have complete control over. Now is the time to create for yourself the life you have always dreamed of having and deserve.

Wishing you all the best of luck!

Contents

Acknowledgments 11
Just a Warm-Up Before We Get Started 13
1. Move-out Strategy Plan and Assessment 17
2. Move-Out Time Frame 28
3. Employment, Social Media and Income 30
4. Professional Grooming and Preparation 39
5. Preparing for the Interview 41
6. Presenting Yourself to the Interviewer 46
7. Establishing a Credit Rating 49
8. Reviewing Your Financial Situation 57
9. Looking for and Qualifying for a New Home 69
10. Landlord Expectations 83
11. Personal Property Item Search 85
12. Real-Life Experiences 92
    - Date Rape and Safety Tips 97
    - Sexual Harassment 99
13. Some Game Changers 101
14. Other Options 110
15. Resource Guide 115
16. Being Homeless 121
17. Human Trafficking 125

Workbook Section

Social Media 133
Preparing for an Interview 135
Interviewer Possible Sample Questions 141

Presenting Yourself to the Interviewer 145
Tracking Log Sheets 147
    Employment Tracking Log 148
    Banking 160
    Credit Building 167
    House Hunting Log 171
Summary 175

Acknowledgments

www.hhs.gov/ash/oah/adolescent-health-topics/reproductive-health/stds.html
Wikihow.com
Fico.com
Teenhelp.com

Just a Warm-Up Before We Get Started

Now that you are ready to start life on your own terms and are planning on moving out as soon as you can, let's take a look at a few things.

Like most adults would do (but some don't), start by making a *really honest assessment* of your options, assets, liabilities, challenges, and whatever else you may need to be considering in making this life-changing decision.

You need to know what to expect in order to make a plan that will succeed. A plan that you can really work to your advantage for your move out to be successful. A plan to make it as smooth of a transition as it can be for you and for your parents or guardians.

Carefully assess if you are really ready to pack your clothes, memorabilia, stereo, TV, and that special teddy bear, pillow, or blanket you have been sleeping with since you were, well, a kid.

You may be considering making this move because you are sick and tired of being told what to do, when to be home, or have had enough of the house rules. Some of you want out and you want out as soon as you can because you have had enough! Others of you are ready to start your own life and feel you are mature enough to do it successfully. Some of you will have no choice but to go out on your own due to other circumstances and will have no support at all. If that is your case, this will be very useful information.

If you are on the fence about making the decision of a lifetime and considering whether to move out or not, what have you been doing to get ready for this *big dive out of the nest*?

Many young adults that leave home and don't go off simply because they want to live in a dormitory at some college, they leave because they want to leave those nagging, advice-tossing, lecturing parents that keep telling them what to do and how to do it. Those parents that want you to check in once in a while and ask too much from you. Those parents that love you and want the best for you. Those parents who don't want you to make the same mistakes they did and want more for you.

Others have shown maturity in their decision to move out, and both kinds of young adults give it a try. (Most secretly want the freedom of doing what they want, whenever they want, not even anything that's out of line. They just want their own place.)

Can your parents stop you from moving out once you are eighteen? *Nope*. Do parents know that if you just left, there is nothing they can do about it? Oh yeah, of course, they know.

There is a difference between the young adults of any family leaving home. The difference is certainly in the maturity level of each young adult that leaves home. Parents will worry either way. However, if a young adult is more mature, a parent may worry just a little bit less, whereas an immature young adult may cause some serious loss of sleep and mental anguish for parents.

There's another difference—the difference between you leaving with their consent and them being proud of how you leave the home you've been raised in. *Leaving without their consent* and just walking out creates hostility and bad feelings for everyone. Certainly, this is not the way to move out. That would be your first of the many big mistakes to come. Especially since you are trying to prove you are ready to live your life as a self-sustaining mature adult.

If you do this the right way, your parents or guardians will do whatever they can to support your success outside of their home. I can guarantee that if you do this the right way, you will be able to ask for help anytime without feeling that you are eating crow or hearing the dreaded "I told you so."

If you move out the wrong way, man up or woman up, and do whatever you can to rebuild some kind of self-respect and have a good communicative relationship with your parents. Asking for help will be so much easier for you if you get on good terms and work together.

If you do not establish and keep a good communicative relationship with your parents, you will always dread the "I told you so" lectures you may possibly get when you are forced to ask for any kind of help.

Making your exit may define your future and what the relationship will be between you and your parents when you walk out the door.

You want to do it the right way.

Let's get you started for the *big dive out of the nest*!

1

Move-out Strategy Plan and Assessment

Preparing Your Move-out Plan and a Few Things You Should Have in Place Before the Big Day

What do you have *of use* right now while you are living at home? Let's go down a list of things and physical items you probably don't realize, but you will certainly need to recognize are pretty nice to have at the tip of your fingers.

Let's look at your current living situation.

These comforts and utility services are currently paid for by your parents and provided to you for free:

- house, condo, or apartment with a bedroom for you to use
- electricity service
- water service
- garbage pickup
- sewer service (Sewer service is needed when you flush the toilet, take a shower, do laundry, etc.)
- natural gas or propane (needed for gas stoves, clothes dryers, and heating)
- cable TV service

- internet service
- septic service (if you live in an area that has no city provided services)

What other things are provided to you right now while you live at home?

All property items, although they are currently provided to you, belong to your parents, not to you.

- groceries
- clothes and shoes
- a bed to sleep in with sheets, blankets, and pillows
- video game component and games
- possibly a nightstand or two, a dresser, lamps, or light fixtures
- maybe a ceiling fan for those hot days and nights (air conditioner?)
- certainly a heater
- bathroom and shower—don't forget, towels, washcloths, soap, shampoo, conditioner, hair dryer, product for your hair, toothbrush, deodorant, toothpaste, comb or brush or even both!
- first-aid things
- ladies' personal items: pads, tampons, etc. (Just something minor for you ladies to think about since they all cost extra money every month. Guys need a few different things of their own).

In the kitchen, you may have use of these appliances:

- microwave
- stove
- refrigerator
- coffeepot
- toaster
- dishwasher
- magic bullet or blender

And maybe a few other miscellaneous appliances.

Oh, don't forget there are also the following:

- pots
- pans
- cooking and serving utensils
- measuring cups
- kitchen sponges and towels
- oven mitts
- hot plate pads
- baking and serving dishes
- spoons, forks, and knives
- plates, bowls, cups, and glasses

And a few other things. Look around and see what else is in a kitchen. You may also have a place to eat, a dining room table and chairs, maybe an eat-in kitchen table or breakfast bar or nook.

Living Room

- TV on a stand or one mounted on the wall (maybe a TV and internet bundle)
- sofa
- love seat
- comfy chair
- maybe a coffee table and end tables with lamps
- window curtains (I am sure you have window coverings in your bedroom too!)
- wall decor and other decorative things

Garage

Most likely, the garage or somewhere in the house there is a washer and dryer to do the laundry. You may also have a bike, surfboard, dirt bike, car parts, and boxes of stuff you just have no room for in your bedroom. Other things you may have available are things like camping equipment or maybe your family owns an RV, motorcycles and/or four-wheelers. Look around, and see what's in there too.

Yard, Patio, or Porch

Your family home may have an area used to entertain or relax:

- lounge or yard furniture
- yard swing
- pool
- hot tub
- barbecue grill

What Else Are You Not Paying for at Home?

Medical insurance:	You may have medical insurance and go to the doctor or ER as needed.
Dental insurance:	You may have dental insurance and go to the dentist as needed.
Eye care:	You may have ophthalmology coverage and go to the eye doctor as needed.
Vehicle:	You may have a car provided by your parents along with auto insurance.
Other transportation:	Your parents may provide funds for alternative transportation like a bus, subway or train.
Cell phone:	You may have a cell phone that they bought for you to use and they pay for monthly.
Laptop or tablet:	You may have a laptop or tablet that they bought for you to use with internet service they pay for.
Vacations:	Your parents may take you on family vacations or to visit friends and family that live far from where you live. The family may have to fly or drive there.
Meals out:	Families enjoy having meals outside of the house after a long week or just to celebrate.

Extra cash: You may currently ask your parents for money when you need a few extra bucks.

What Do You Get from Living at Home That You Don't Pay for?

Parents may

- do your laundry;
- clean the house;
- do grocery shopping;
- pay the house bills;
- take care of you if you are sick;
- cook your meals, breakfast, lunch, dinner and provide snacks;
- pay for your new clothes;
- pay for your cell phone;
- pay for your iPad or tablet service bills;
- give you money when you need it;
- pay for car registration;
- pay for vacations;
- pay for other miscellaneous extras you don't notice.

Will You Be Ready to Pay for All These Things and Your New Living Expenses?

So far, you seem to have everything, possibly including a few chores and responsibilities, like cleaning your room, taking out the trash, mowing the lawn, helping keep the garage, house, and kitchen clean, along with getting home when you are told. Some of you are even expected or required to attend family functions and gatherings.

For most of you, those house rules are really tough, and you want to move out and do whatever you want. Again, once you are eighteen, you can go. They can't stop you or do a thing about it, and you know it and they know it, and they can change the locks.

What else happens when you turn eighteen? The law also now considers you an adult too. Big surprise, right?

Any legal issues you have will be on your record for many years, depending on the issue. Legal actions that have severe consequences may show up on reports when you apply for home or apartment rentals and when you apply for jobs, therefore reducing *greatly* what kind of employer will hire you and who will allow you rent if you have a criminal record. (Most companies and employers are now checking criminal records before renting to new tenants and employers before hiring a new employee).

Money Burners

What do you think that means? Many young adults have been burning money for most of their lives. What is burning money? Burning money is the way many people, not just young adults, are negligent and wasteful in the way they live because they may not fork out money to pay those bills. For example, look at the household grocery bill, electricity bill and water bill, just to name a few.

Money Burner #1 Grocery bill

Be conscious of the groceries for a few days or weeks. Ask to see the receipts after the shopping. Then, be aware of YOUR habits. Half eaten sandwiches, partially consumed drinks, food that you may have taken to your room and not finish that gets thrown away and, my all time favorite, sitting down for a meal and feeling so hungry that you pile on the food like a small mountain, only to eat very little of it. What about the rest of the food? Yep, trash or garbage disposal.....money burned!

What about friends coming over? Yep, when no one is home or even when someone is home, the raiding of the kitchen typically happens. Money burned feeding friends. It will look a lot different when it is YOU buying those groceries.

Quick quiz: Look at the receipt for groceries, look up the minimum wage the city allows for salaries, deduct a few bucks, (taxes employers will take out before you get your pay check) and divide the hourly wage, (minus the few bucks), by the cost shown on the grocery bill receipt. How many hours of work would it have taken to buy those groceries? Would it have taken one, two or three days of work to have paid for that grocery run? Everything tossed in the grocery cart adds up!

Money Burner #2 Electricity Bill

Burning money is when anything related to electricity is left on and when it's not being used. When lights are on and no one is in the room, the radio is left on, computer is running, and whatever else is plugged in that uses electricity. Go outside and look at the electricity meter, every move that little rotating pointer makes or digital reader increases is money that has to be paid. And believe me it adds up! What's worse? When negligently the air conditioner is on and the doors and/or windows are open or fans are left on to cool the house. That electricity reading meter will run forever and ever, making that electricity bill skyrocket.

Yep, some things do have to run 24/7, like the refrigerator, most built in microwaves that have clocks, some stoves with clocks and some household clocks. Almost everyone carries a cell phone 24/7 and can check the time, so those built in clocks are money burners! A few other things are money burners like the TV, cable boxes, internet, and answering machines. They are not using tons of electricity, but, it all adds up!

Quick quiz: Look at the electricity bill, look up the minimum wage the city allows for salaries, deduct a few bucks, (taxes employers will take out before you get your pay check) and divide the hourly wage, (minus the few bucks), by the cost shown on the electricity bill. How many hours of work would it have taken you to pay for that bill? Would it have taken you one, two or three days to pay that electricity bill? Everything you leave on will cost money!

Money Burner #3 Water bill.

It can be pricey to run water, especially in areas that experience droughts. For example, 30 minute showers, what does it cost per shower? In draught controlled areas, that could be pretty expensive per shower and to shower once per day each year, the cost is about $3,900 per year for a family of four. The water bill can be reduced if time in the shower can AVERAGE 10–11 minutes.

The cost is a little higher to run the water until it gets to someone's liking, typically about 5 minutes, to run the water to heat it up for 5 minutes and add the extra cost for a total of $2.75 per shower in some areas. To be fair, no one likes a cold shower. Again, cost varies depending on the city, state or country.

Take some time and be more aware of where money goes, how it is spent in your household and how you spend your money. Once you live on your own, you will definitely keep a very close eye on every penny you earn.

Reminds me of a television show where the son moves out of his parents' house and gets his own apartment. Dad waits for him to get all settled in and then pops over for a visit. Son proudly tells dad to make himself at home, that he has to step out of the house for a little bit and when he returns, the windows are all open, the air conditioner is on full blast, all the lights are on in every room, the television is on in the living room and in the bedroom, dad has kicked off his shoes and one is in the hall and the other in the middle of the living room, his jacket is tossed in a corner and dad has opened several cans of drinks and placed them throughout the house along with a few glasses of water. He has also opened bags of snacks, chips and cookies and had some on the dining room table, coffee table and end table. Son returns and is really freaked out and starts closing windows, turning off lights, collecting full cans and the food and snacks. He starts complaining to his dad.

Son is in complete disbelief!

Dad, what are you doing? He asks. Dad grins and says. Making myself at home like you told me to. Isn't this how you made yourself at home when you lived with your mother and me? This is what you have been doing to us for years and it has cost us a fortune.

Why am I telling this story? Because it is exactly how many young adults live. It's taken for granted that everything is there to use without consideration for what it costs and who pays for it. Typically these things are paid for by parents or guardians.

After doing the financial worksheet sections and budgets if you realize that you can't afford to move out at this time, here are a few suggestions to earn some adult points and respect: Stop being the kid in the house. This means earn some adult respect. It means not expecting to behave like an irresponsible, disrespectful person and demand to be treated like the adult you want to be seen as. How can this be done? Accept that life is different now. If you are 18, they can kick you out, so you want to be a better compromiser. You have to take care of yourself, your clothes, cleaning up and doing what every other adult does:

- Without being told, bathe, brush your teeth and wear clean clothes. You can keep your own style, but be neat and clean about it.
- Wash your own dishes after you eat. Don't leave them there to "do later". That is an expectation that someone else will do them. Offer to help clean up after meals. The kitchen gets cleaned faster if more people are helping.
- Do your own laundry. If you don't know how, ask your parents, a friend or look it up on a You Tube video.

- Keep your room clean. Make your bed. Keep things off the floor, and get it to smell fresh by opening some windows. (or a little bit of air freshener will go a long way).
- Use good manners. Please and thank you will get you lots of respect. Show gratitude.
- Ask your parents or guardians for a list of house responsibilities you can take over to "earn" your place in the house. After all, you are not paying rent, electrical bills, water bills, cable, internet or groceries.

This shows you are becoming more responsible, taking initiative and getting ready by earning the respect you will want and will deserve. The difference in how you are seen and treated by your parents or guardians will be noticeable.

Keep in mind that once you are 18, you are now a guest in their house. You are a legal adult and if they choose, they may ask you to leave. If you will be staying in the house for now, remember that it is not a hotel, you don't have a taxi service, cook, maid or laundry attendant.

Don't disrespect your family home by boozing it up secretly in your room or doing drugs. Don't have overnight guests unless it has been discussed and agreed to. Keep in mind, every guest costs money (Lights, water, food etc).

Be respectful of their house, their rules and what they pay for until you have enough money to do it on your own.

You may have a conversation with them and discuss where you all stand and how this can be a good experience and even agree to some household rules.

Try really hard not to treat them like an ATM machine, and if you are going out, let them know approximately when you will return. Parents will still worry about you every time you are out and they hear sirens, screeching tires and ambulances go by. If they are watching TV, and hear of auto accidents, they will check to make sure you were not in that accident.

If you have a job and your intention is to move out, make sure your parents know you have this goal. Instead of paying rent, let them know you would like to put money in the bank to start getting ready for that move out. They will understand.

Being an adult means that once you're eighteen, absolutely everything you do counts.

2

Move-Out Time Frame

If you have made your decision and are still *really determined about moving on*, are you ready?

Keep reading to figure out if you can handle the financial responsibility, if you are ready to move out and what you will need to do in order to get ready.

In choosing to take the big dive from the nest, it's best to prepare yourself. Your preparation should start, at minimum, a year or two in advance. During that time, consider putting these things in place:

- the move-out plan
- employment
- driver's license and secondary photo ID (photo ID from DMV, passport, or birth certificate)
- transportation (If you own a reliable vehicle, make sure you have auto insurance).
- bank account(s) (checking and saving accounts opened and some money in each account)
- established credit (There is a credit section coming up).

- money to cover deposits, moving expenses, and living expenses
- some idea about where you will rent and the cost of your new rental
- renter's insurance (You can get it for a low price with same the company that provides your auto insurance).
- inventory of household supplies and items you own and will take with you
- inventory of what you need to buy or get
- list of weekly, monthly, quarterly, and yearly expenses (This is coming up too).
- list of companies that will provide you services, i.e., electric, water, garbage, cable, internet, phone, etc.
- handy list of other resources you may need

3

Employment, Social Media and Income

(with Sample Cover Letter, Resumé, and Employment Application)

If you have a job, you have passed your first hurdle. The job you have will help. You can start saving money while you live at home and are not paying for anything. You will want to be earning enough money to be able to afford your new life. (You are going to need the money, believe me)! How much money you need will be discussed later.

If you don't have a job yet, please consider a couple of things. Get some help in preparing for an interview with possible employers and know how to dress accordingly for an interview. No employer wants to see sagging pants, wrinkled clothing, un-kept hair, and dirty shoes. If you have body art, long sleeves are a great idea when going in for a job interview. Unless you will be interviewed by an employer that you know is fine with exposed body art, wear long sleeves. Use good manners. *Please* and *thank you* go a long way too! You will be a representative of their business, so know how to dress the part.

Possible Employment Documentation Requirements

Everywhere you fill out applications, regardless of what the application is for, the company reviewing it may also require some form of documentation and the following:

- resumé
- employment application
- driver's license or photo identification (passport or ID from DMV)
- social security card
- birth certificate
    * possible drug testing
    * possible competency testing
    * possible health and physical screening
    * If you are going to drive a company vehicle, you may need to provide a copy of your driving record. (You can get it at DMV. There may be a small fee).

Drug Use

Most jobs require drug testing these days. Chances are, if you are using drugs, you will not be hired by any company that tests for drug use if you pop dirty. If you are on prescribed medication, bring in your prescription so that it may be reviewed when the drug screening takes place. Although many states have legalized marijuana, employers may not be accepting of this drug on a drug screening for a job. Being drug free opens up all kinds of opportunities. Being a drug user for recreational or medical use closes many doors and windows of opportunity, some because of employer personal preference, others for the safety and security of the company and staff.

Social Media

We all love social media; so do employers. Be aware that, these days, the human resources department of most companies want to know what kind of person you are besides what you are telling them on your resumé. Most of them are Googling you and looking around the internet to find out more about you, especially if they want to hire you. What you post online may get you the job or cost you the job.

Income

Know about your income. Learn how to read a pay stub. You will, very quickly, learn when you see your paycheck, the difference between your gross pay and your net pay. Just to give you a little bit of information, your gross pay is what you are paid *before* your deductions are taken from your salary. Deductions are taken from your paycheck before you are given a paycheck with what is left. What is left is called net pay. What are typical deductions for? The government has standard deductions like social security, Medicare, state taxes, and federal taxes, just to name a few. Employees may also have deductions for medical insurance, dental insurance, long-term care insurance, 401(k) retirement, and whatever else may be required or necessary by law, or any other deductions you request.

Banking

As soon as you become employed and get your first paycheck, head over to your preferred bank or credit union and open a checking and/or savings account. You may want to research bank and credit union fees regarding costs to use ATMs, writing checks, and what other miscellaneous fees they will charge you. (These are typically taken out of your account automatically every month when statements are sent out). Do this before selecting who you will bank with. Most have monthly fees and minimum balances they want to see in your account at all times. Go to the banks or credit unions, or just look online for where you will save the most money. Yes, they charge you money to hold on to your money!

Banking Credit Card and Debit Card Side Note

Businesses charge extra fees when you use your debit or credit cards. Many bank ATMs that are not associated with *your* selected bank or credit union may charge additional fees when you withdraw cash from your accounts. Research and know what it will cost for you to have a credit card and bank account. Know the fees and interest rates you will be charged. It's your money. Don't give it away by not understanding how the banking system works and makes money from you.

Cover Letter Sample

Your name
Email address
Phone number

Date

Interviewer's name
Title of interviewer (if you know it)
Company name
Address
City, state, zip code

Dear Mr./Mrs./Ms. _______________:

#1—In this paragraph, you tell why you are writing. You want to get their attention and get them interested in *you* as an employee. You might want to show them that you know their company. (Look them up on the Internet and get to know as much about them as possible, and sell yourself). Write it in three to four sentences only.

#2—Tell them about your qualifications, the job you are interested in, and why you think you are the best choice for this job.

#3—In this paragraph, you are going to tell them about your education and the skills you have that qualify you for the job. If you don't have a lot of work experience, you can tell them about extracurricular activities that you are involved in that would relate to the job.

#4—The final paragraph is used to thank the person for his/her time and consideration.

Sincerely,

Sign your name here

Type out your name here

Resumé Sample

Your first and last name
Your email address
Home: 555-666-7777 Cell: 888-999-0000

Summary
Student with a great interest in photography. Extensive experience in photography on all types of subjects. Praised and awarded for photographs taken and entered in photography contests.

Education
Name of your high school, city, state, and zip code
High school diploma to be received in June 20XX (if you have graduated, date of graduation)
GPA 3.86, honor roll student
Electives: photography, creative writing
Activities: tennis, football, chess

Volunteer and Community Service (if any)
Name and address of volunteer location
Your position
Spring 20XX–present

- Use bullet points, in this format, on what you did as a volunteer.
- Name something you did.
- Name something else you did.
- If you got any awards or recognition, name it here too.

Using this same format, add all your job or volunteer experiences. If you have none, leave this section out of your resumé.

Certification(s)
List all your certifications here. CPR and AED Certification, April 20XX

Application for Employment Sample

Personal information:
Date of application: ____________________
Name: ____________________
Address: ____________________
____
Phone: (___)______________ Email: ____________________
How did you learn about our company? ____________________
Position sought: ____________ Available start date: ____________
Desired pay range: __________ Are you currently employed? _______
Education: ______________ High school graduate? Yes __ No ___
If yes, what high school? ________ College graduate? Yes __ No __
If yes, what college did you graduate from? ____________________
What was your major? _________ College or university: _________

Other education:
Please list any specialized training and trade schools. Also, list your areas of highest proficiency, special skills, or other items that may contribute to your abilities in performing the above-mentioned position.

____
____
____
____
____

Previous experience: (Please list beginning from most recent first.)
Dates of employment: from ____________ to ____________
Company: ________________ Address: ________________
Name of supervisor: ____________________ Phone: ____________
Position: ___________ Special skills used: ____________________
Reason for leaving: ____________________
Dates of employment: from ____________ to ____________
Company: ________________ Address: ________________
Name of supervisor: ____________________ Phone: _________

Position:______________________Special skills used:_______________
Reason for leaving:

____

____

____

Dates of employment: from ________________ to _________________
Company:___________________Address:_______________________
Name of supervisor: __________ Phone: ________________________
Position: _____________________ Special skills used: _______________
Reason for leaving:

____

____

____

Dates of employment: from ________________ to _________________
Company:___________________Address:_______________________
Name of supervisor: __________ Phone: ________________________
Position: _____________________ Special skills used: _______________
Reason for leaving:

____

____

____

May we contact your current employer? Yes __________ No _______

I declare that the statements above are true and correct. I hereby give authorization to ABC Employer to verify all information provided in this application. Permission is granted to contact previous employers, to check criminal record, court records, income, bank account, and credit information. I understand that providing false, misleading or incomplete information will result in employment being denied.

Applicant signature___________________ Date____________________
Applicant signature___________________ Date____________________
Company HR rep signature ___________ Date ____________________

Important note when filling out online applications, carefully review the job description and requirements. Use key words from their own description on your online application. Today's online SEO's (Search Engine Optimizers) look for key words in the online application to sort out which applications will be reviewed and which applications will never been seen.

4

Professional Grooming and Preparation

Gentlemen, you want to look professional:

- Once freshly showered, deodorant applied, properly groomed, and with every hair in place, select clothing that is in line with the company. Select a clean suit (tie is optional unless the company is of that caliber) or neatly ironed clothes, clean pair of slacks with a collared shirt, and a crisp-looking belt with dress shoes. (Socks should complement the color of your shoes.)
- Do not show up for an interview in baggy or saggy jeans no matter how clean they are. Don't wear sneakers, flip-flops, T-shirts, sweatshirts, or inappropriate clothing.
- Don't wear strong scented colognes that linger after you have left the room.

Ladies, for a professional look:

- Once freshly showered, deodorant applied, properly groomed, and with every hair in place, select clothing that is in line with the company. Wear a clean and pressed pant-suit or skirt suit (depending on the caliber of the company).

- Select an outfit that looks professional, not provocative. No plunging necklines, miniskirts, heels that are too high, or colors and patterns that are too much out of the realm of the setting you are going to work in. No chipped nail polish or crazy nail polish colors and patterns.
- Select your makeup carefully when getting ready for your interview. Select and use conservative, clean, and professional-looking colors.
- Don't wear strong scented perfumes that linger after you have left the room.

Side note for men and women: If you have those beautiful tattooed sleeves, I recommend you wear a long-sleeved shirt to your interview until you know about the body art policy for the company.

5

Preparing for the Interview

Before going on any interview, look up the company. Learn about it and what its business mission is. Regardless of how menial it may seem, employers are impressed with the fact that you took time to learn about their business and its details.

Look at the announcement for the position that you are applying for, and be familiar with what you will say that best describes why you would be the best person for the job.

Look up cover letter samples that you can use as guides to prepare a cover letter, specifically in the name of the interviewer if you know the person's name or to the hiring manager if you don't know who will be interviewing you. Cover letter should only be a couple of short paragraphs.

Look up sample resumés that you can use as guides, and prepare a resumé. Print out two to four copies of your cover letter and resumé. Have someone look over your cover letter and resumé, and check for errors. You will want to hand one of each to the interviewer so you can follow along with your own copy in hand. Present your cover letter on top of your resumé.

Prepare and print a list of questions you have for the interviewer. You will want to be able to look at your list in case some of the questions were not answered.

Arrive ten minutes early for your interview. Leave your cell phone in the car or turn it off. *Do not* put it on vibrate mode because it may still make noise during the interview.

Below you will find some questions you can ask. Feel free to add any of your own questions or leave out any that will not apply. Place your cover letter, resumé, and list of questions in an easy-to-access case or folder. (Do not take your papers in a backpack).

Be prepared to tell the interviewer a little bit about yourself, at some point, during your interview. Look the interviewer in the eye, and share main points about yourself. Sell yourself as if you were your favorite product.

Be prepared to answer interviewer questions such as:

- Why did you apply for this job?
- Have you applied at other places? If so, where?
- Do you have transportation to get to work? If so, what is your means of transportation?
- Are you available weekdays, evenings, and weekends?
- How soon can you start if you are hired?
- Why should we hire you?

Job Insight

There may be other questions directly related to the position you are applying for. That's why you should research the company and find out how you can make yourself the *best* choice. Sell yourself through your leisure activities, school activities, personal experiences, and how they all mesh into the experience they are looking for.

Are you applying at a fast food place or restaurant? If you like to cook, grill barbecue, help in the kitchen, or just enjoy cooking, use that as a selling point.

Are you applying for a data-entry or computer-related position? If you are proficient on your computer, specify the programs you use most and programs that can be associated with that position. State them.

You get the picture?

What Questions Should You Ask and When Should You Ask?

During the interview, some of the questions on the following list will be answered for you. The interviewer will ask you if you have any questions once he or she is finished explaining the job to you. Some of the answers to these questions may have been on the job opening announcement. (Depending on the job, select what questions you may want to ask and add some of your own questions).

Some basic questions you can choose to ask are as follows:

- Is this a full-time or part-time position? (unless stated in the job description)
- Is there training involved? (unless stated in the job description)
- Is there a probationary period? If so, how long is it?
- What are the working hours?
- Are the workdays flexible?
- Does the company have paid holidays?
- Does the company offer paid sick days?
- What is the salary for this position? (unless stated in the job description)
- What benefits come with the position? (i.e., vacation, medical, dental, 401(k))
- Is this a company I can grow with?
- Is there anything else I should know?
- How soon will you make a decision and fill the position?

*If you are available to start right away, say it. Show your enthusiasm!

Before interviewing, review the "Workbook Section," then you will be ready to head out the door for your interview.

Leave home early so you will not be late. Try to be there about ten minutes before your scheduled interview time.

Once you arrive, check in with the person at the desk, door, counter, or office window.

Politely tell them your full name, why you are there, and who you are there to see. For example, I would say, "Good afternoon. I'm Jamie Job Seeker. I have an appointment for an interview with the Hiring Manager at 1:30 today."

Once you have checked in, you may be asked to take a seat and wait or you will be escorted to the interview office or room. Do not be on your cell phone while waiting to be interviewed.

Try to relax even though you may be a little nervous.

6

Presenting Yourself to the Interviewer

If you are escorted into an office or room and the interviewer is present, introduce yourself as you shake hands. Have a firm handshake, but don't make the interviewer say uncle. Look the interviewer in the eye and show self-confidence.

If the interviewer asks you to take a seat, do so, and take out a copy of your cover letter and resumé. Hand them to the interviewer with the cover letter on top. You can say this is your first job interview and that you are a little nervous. They understand; they were once in your seat too.

Don't fidget or be looking around the room, and sit up straight in your seat, don't slouch. Focus on the interviewer. Keep your eyes on that person, and listen attentively.

When the interviewer is explaining about the company and the position, he or she may stop to ask if you have any questions about what was just explained. If you don't understand, ask questions. Do not assume.

Take a quick glance at your questions sheet, and ask any questions that were not answered and you still want to ask.

The End of the Interview

Once the interview is over and you both stand up, *as you are shaking hands*, you may want to say something like: "Thank you for your time. I appreciate the opportunity to interview with you about this position. I hope you will seriously consider me for the job. I promise to give my best effort if I am selected."

You can do this!

*Super Helpful Hint: Send a Thank You Card

On your way home, stop and get a thank you card. When you get home, sit down, handwrite a note to the interviewer, and mail it *at once*!

It should say something like:

> Dear Mr. Hiring Manager, <--put the interviewer's name here.
>
> I'd like to thank you for taking the time to interview me for the position of _________ at your company. I look forward to hearing from you very soon and, hopefully, becoming part of your team.
>
> Sincerely yours,
> Sign your name here

Income (This paragraph is intentionally repeated.)

Know about your income. Learn how to read your pay stub. You will very quickly learn when you see your paycheck, the difference between your gross pay and your net pay.

Just to give you a little bit of information, your gross pay is what you are paid before required deductions are taken from your salary. Deductions are taken from your paycheck before you are given a paycheck with what is left. What is left is called net pay.

What are these deductions for? The city, state, and federal government (IRS) have standard deductions like social security, Medicare, city taxes, state taxes, and federal taxes, just to name a few. Employees may also have deductions for medical insurance, dental insurance, long-term care insurance, 401(k) Retirement, (sometimes this one is optional), and whatever else may be required or necessary by law, and any other deductions you request.

7

Establishing a Credit Rating

A good credit score will be required for almost everything you do.

What is a credit score?

What companies determine a credit score?

What's a FICO score?

Why does someone need a credit score?

Who has to have one?

How does someone establish credit?

How does a credit score affect renting or buying a home and getting a loan or applying for credit?

Anyone who wants to *ever* rent, lease, or purchase anything by getting a loan needs established credit. A good credit score is the only way to get financial help.

What is a credit score? (not the same as your FICO score, also explained in this section) It's a number-rating system that reports how a consumer (you and I) pay his or her bills and what is reported to the credit-monitoring companies by people that extend credit to a consumer.

Here is the rating scale:

- Excellent Credit: 781–850
- Good Credit: 661–780
- Fair Credit: 601–660
- Poor Credit: 501–600
- Bad Credit: below 500

Who determines a credit score?

The following are the three credit reporting companies that will monitor your paying habits and maintain your credit for the rest of your life: Equifax, Experian, and TransUnion.

Once you get the ball rolling and start establishing the credit history you will need, you will want to become familiar with these companies, how to read a credit report, how to make changes to your report, and how it will affect your life.

Why does someone need a credit score?

A credit score is needed if someone wants to get a loan for anything. For example, if you want to buy a car, unless you have several thousands of dollars to buy it with cash, you will need a loan. In order to get a loan to buy that car, you need to have established credit. In order to rent or lease a home, vehicle, or anything else outside of cash you may have on hand, you will want to make sure you have good established credit that shows bills are paid on time and that the applicant, you, are a good loan risk. A good credit rating is typically required.

Prior to hiring someone to join their team of employees, many employers now check an applicant's credit report and also order background checks, especially if the applicant will be handling money and/or have access to personal information, other property, confidential information about the company and its clients.

Who has to have one?

Anyone who ever wants to borrow money needs a credit score. Some smaller independent companies don't require a credit report, but they will charge *very* high repayment interest rates as a trade-off for the risk of your not having credit. Beware of the *small print* and specifics of any agreement you are signing to get a loan. Keep in mind, once you sign, *you are fully responsible for what they put in writing and you agree to by signing.* (It's a good idea to have someone else review the agreement with you before you sign it, not them. They want you to sign it)!

How does a credit score affect getting a loan?

An Excellent Credit score, 781–850, will get you the best interest rates, highest credit card rewards, and pretty much makes you a "golden client." In lender terms, your great credit means you are an "A paper" client. This means you can get loans from just about any company or bank where you apply for loans or credit cards. It means you are great at paying your bills on time and are a very financially responsible client.

A Good Credit score, 661–780, will still get you a decent interest rate. You will still be offered credit by several companies with this credit score. Credit card companies and banks will increase rates when extending loans to someone with a Good Credit score, and cap credit card spending availability limits.

Periodically review your credit rating, speak to a customer service representative where you have your credit cards or loans, and ask for a review for an adjustment on your interest rate. Fixed agreements will not make adjustments unless you refinance (i.e., a car loan, mortgage, or fixed-term loan agreement).

With a Fair Credit score 601–660, you are a risk for a loan. Loans offered to you will have higher interest rates, and there will be nothing you can do about it, except improve your credit over a time period by paying your bills on time and keeping your balances as low as possible.

Poor Credit, 501–600, and Bad Credit, 500 and below, are about the same in any creditor's point of view. They are the *highest* loan risk and *very* few companies—possibly no banks or credit unions, no auto dealerships, and no credit card companies—will offer you credit. The best thing to do is work on improving this credit score.

More and more people are extending credit to Poor Credit applicants at *loan shark* rates. This means that you can borrow money, and you will pay almost illegally high interest rates to borrow it. Chances are that you will *never* be able to pay it back because the interest is so high that every payment you make will barely pay the interest alone.

* Every person starts off with no credit. It takes about six months to establish a credit history and get a credit score. As time goes by and you continue to use your credit cards responsibly, you will see your credit score rise. As your credit score gets into higher ranges, more credit may become available to you and at better terms and interest rates. When using your access to credit, keep this tip in mind: *only apply for credit that you need and always pay your bills on time.*

How to Establish Credit

Establishing your credit can start at a very young age.

Understand your credit card limit: The limit is the maximum amount of money you can charge to your credit card account. Since it is your first credit card, your limit may be anywhere from $200–1,500 or maybe a little more. If you have a high limit, don't be impressed with yourself; you need to be more careful not to use the *limit*. Don't spend your credit card to its limit.

Monthly payments: Know when your payments are due. If you have late payments, you will have a late payment fee and a ding on your credit, and it will lower your credit score. If you pay only the minimum due, it may also lower your credit score. Add a few extra dollars with every payment for an improved credit score.

Interest rates and how are they charged: Every company giving out loans charges an interest rate for the convenience of using their money. High interest rates are bad. If your credit comes with a 10% interest rate and you charge a purchase on your card for $500, you can get $50 interest charge and have to pay back $550. That is not a good trade-off for a credit card.

* Usually, if you don't pay back the balance in full, you will start to pay interest on the amount you have not paid back. For example, your balance is $500 and you pay $250. Check your interest rate. If your yearly interest rate is 12%, you're going to pay 1% each month: $500 - $250 = $250 x .01 = $2.5 for that month.

* Look for a low APR credit card. APR stands for Annual Percentage Rate. It's the rate associated with the card similar to that discussed above. If an APR is 20%, and you charge $1,000 on your card, you will have to pay back $1,000 x .20 = $200 in interest on your card. That's $1,200 for the privilege of spending $1,000. Think of it as renting money.

*How to manage and understand the best use of your credit card for the best credit rating, and credit utilization: Another phrase for this is "Debt-to-Ratio Limit." This means that it's a comparison of how much you owe to how much total debt you carry. For credit cards, you want a low credit utilization. For example, if you have $300 of debt on your credit cards and your total limit is $600, you get your credit utilization by *dividing* your debt with your limit. Divide $300 by $600 = .5 = 50%. This 50% is a pretty high credit utilization. If you have $100 of debt on your credit card and your total limit is $1,000, your credit card utilization is $100 divided by $1,000 = .10 = 10%. This 10% is a great credit utilization.

A great credit utilization is 10% of your available credit. The average credit utilization is 25–30%. If you are in that range, you're still doing really well.

*Once you have applied for a credit card, wait about six months before applying for a second card. One way to increase your credit score is to have two cards and use one of them regularly. There are advantages and disadvantages to this strategy.

Advantage: Your total credit limit goes up. If you have a credit card with a $500 credit limit and you apply and get another credit card with a $500 credit limit, you have doubled your credit limit by having two credit cards and now have a $1,000 credit limit. The higher your credit limits and the lower your balances, the higher your credit score will be.

Disadvantage: If you haven't established good credit yet, your credit will take a hit if you apply for a second credit card too soon. Wait about a year before applying for a second card (wikiHow information).

Another way to establish credit is to apply for a secure credit card. Secure credit cards are used to establish credit using a savings account at your bank. The bank will allow you to put your cash into an account that is locked into the secured credit card and ensure that if you don't pay your credit card bill, the bank may use that account to cover your balance. If the bank takes this avenue, your credit will be dinged and credit score lowered. The money in the saving account cannot be withdrawn or used as long as that secured credit card is active.

There are several lenders out there that advertise to help you get credit. *Beware* of their contracts and their *super-duper high* interest rates. If it's too good to be true, it can't be good. Do not apply for more than two credit cards within the first year. When you apply for your first card, be sure to make all payments on time in order to establish a good paying history. Wait at least 6 months before applying for your second card.

What Is a FICO Score?

The name FICO comes from the company's original name, the Fair Isaac Co. It was often shortened to FICO and, finally, became the company's official name several years ago.

To create credit scores, they use information provided by one of the three major credit reporting agencies—Equifax, Experian, or TransUnion. But FICO itself is not a credit-reporting agency.

Though FICO scores are the most widely used among lenders, there are other scores lenders can choose from, such as the Vantage Score, which is becoming more widely used.

What Goes into a FICO Score?

There are five main factors that go into FICO scores, and they each have a different effect on your score. Here's the breakdown:

- payment history (35% of the FICO score)
- debt/amounts owed (30%)
- age of credit history (15%)
- new credit/inquiries (10%)
- mix of accounts/types of credit (10%)

All these factors are considered in other credit score models, so it's safe to say that if you have a strong FICO score, you likely have a good score with other models as well. However, for some people, the weight of these categories can vary. For example, people who haven't been using credit for very long will be factored differently than those with a longer credit history, according to FICO. So the importance of any one of these factors depends on the overall information in your credit report.

That's why it's a good idea to not get too hung up on the specific number of your credit score. Instead, focus on what areas of your credit are strong and which ones you might want to work on (FICO information by Credit.com).

Banking (intentionally repeated)

As soon as you become employed and get your first paycheck, head over to your preferred bank or credit union and open a checking and/or savings account. Before selecting whom you will bank with, you may want to research bank and credit union fees regarding the costs to use ATMs, writing checks, and what other miscellaneous fees they will charge you when you become their client. (These are typically taken out of your account automatically every month and show up on your statement as deductions when statements are sent out). Many have monthly fees and minimum balances they want to see in your account at all times. But it isn't necessary. Go to the banks or credit unions, or just look online for where you will save the most money. Yes, they charge you money to hold on to your money!

Banking, Credit Card, and Debit Card Side Note

Businesses charge extra fees when you use your debit or credit cards. Many bank ATMs that are not associated with *your* selected bank may charge additional fees when you withdraw cash from your accounts. Research and know what it will cost you to have a credit card and bank account. Know the fees and interest rates you will be charged and what you will pay for keeping money in their banks and credit unions. It's your money. Don't give it away by not understanding how the banking system works and makes money from you.

Your credit is critical forever.

8

Reviewing Your Financial Situation

First of all, understanding the basics about how much money and personal effort you will need to make this all happen and what it all means consists of a lot of different things. One of the important ones is to keep a cool temperament when negotiating, interviewing, and talking to the people who may be able to help you.

Your approach and personality are critical. Your temperament and manners may be deciding factors in someone deciding whether you get what you are asking for or if you will be rejected.

Moving on.

What is moving out and being on your own all about? It's about growing up and being your own person. In deciding, you have grown up enough to move out and be on your own. Here are a few things you will need to help you out as you get started.

Look at these things carefully. They will help you understand your financial needs better and get you ready for your move out. The list below is associated with getting a new rental home and what you may need or what may be required to move out.

Be financially prepared. Deposits vary depending on where you live.

- Rental deposit: This is typically the same as one month's rent.

First month's rent: Sometimes landlords ask for first and last month's rent This is equal to two months of the rent needed to move in in addition to the deposit above. This would be equivalent to three months of rent.

- Electricity deposit: Call the local electricity provider and ask what the electricity service start-up requires.
- Water deposit: If you rent an apartment, find out if this is included. If it's not, call the local water company and ask what the service start-up requires. Most house rentals typically do not include water service, and you will have to pay for it. Again, deposits *vary* depending on where you live.
- Garbage pickup: If it's not included in your rental or lease agreement, ask who the service is provided by, seek out the provider, call to find out if there is a deposit, how much it is and what the monthly fee will be, and if they provide disposal and recycle cans. Again, if you rent a house, you may be paying this monthly expense.
- Cable and internet deposits: Lots of choices here for companies to use. Deposits depend on who you select for your service and what you select as part of your service contract. **May require a signed contract. Read it carefully and know exactly what you are agreeing to!*

Now you know what to do in order to figure out how much money you will need for deposits just to secure your own place.

Let's get started on the good stuff.

Deposits

First of all, estimate your *deposits* as closely as possible and what is required *just* to move in to a new place. These are *not* part of your monthly expenses.

Rental deposit/first month $__________ (add last month's rent if required)

Electricity deposit $__________

Water deposit $__________

Cable and Internet deposit $__________

Add anything else that needs a deposit $__________

Total deposits needed to move in $__________

Housing Expenses

Basic bills you *will pay every month* for your new place:

Housing
Rent $__________
Electricity $__________
Water $__________
(Sewer typically is included in a water bill, double-check and make sure if it is or not.)
Garbage pickup $__________
Cable, internet, landline $__________
Total monthly housing expenses $__________

In addition to the above, you will have to pay other things too.

Living Expenses

Estimate realistically what these costs may be as follows:

Groceries (per week x 4 or 5 weeks) $________________
Toiletries, as needed (toilet paper, etc.) $________________
Laundry money (if no washer and dryer) $________________
Car payment (or transportation fare, monthly)$________________
Road service (example, AAA, can be monthly) $________________
Gas for the vehicle (per week x 4 or 5 weeks) $________________
Auto insurance (if needed, monthly) $________________
Cell phone (monthly) $________________
Medical insurance $________________
Dental insurance $________________

Total monthly living expenses $________________

Side note: As needed, you may have to save for being able to buy new clothes or money in case the car needs repair or other things come up.

Transportation Expenses

Additional quarterly and yearly required automobile fees that may be needed if you will have a vehicle:

Vehicle maintenance (quarterly oil changes) $________________
Auto registration (due every year) $________________
Auto insurance renewal fee $________________
Total additional fees required $________________

This is money you will need to have saved or you will need to come up with when these payments are due.

The Quick Math

Here is what your new financial life may look like (see explanation of costs and enter totals estimated from previous pages):

Total from deposits
Deposits only $_______ This is the approximate amount of money needed just to secure a new place to live. They are one-time deposits that may be refunded to you when you move out or close out services provided. Deposits are held to cover damages, unpaid bills, or unpaid rents. Upon move out or closing of services, provider has a specific amount of time to provide you with an itemized statement of charges and/or a check for your refund.

Total from housing expenses
Monthly housing expenses $_____________ This is the approximate amount of money you will pay *every month* to keep your new home. This does not include any luxuries.

Total from living expenses
Living expenses $___________ These are necessary expenses to take care of yourself once you are living on your own. They are expenses associated with everyday living.

Total from transportation expenses (additional)
Transportation fees $____________ These are fees that may have to be paid once a year and/or about every quarter if you have a vehicle (oil changes or other auto maintenance as needed).

How Does It Look So Far?

Let's move on and see the big picture.

Here's the amount of money you need to secure a new place to live (separate from, but in addition to, housing, living, and transportation expenses. One-time move-in money needed):

Move-in deposits $ ____________

Balancing of your *monthly* income versus your new future expenses:

Housing total $ ____________
Living expenses total $ ____________
Housing and living monthly total $ ____________
Transportation expenses (only if you own an automobile):
Quarterly/yearly total $ ____________

Final Reality Check

*Move-in refundable money (For home only). $ ________

Again, this money has nothing to do with what you will pay monthly. It is only the amount you will need to move out of your parents' house and *get into a new place of your own*. If you leave your rental in good condition, you may get this money refunded.

Ongoing Monthly Living Expenses

Enter your monthly *net income*	$ + ________
Subtract housing and living from income	$ - ________
Subtract transportation fee, if applicable (1/12)	$ - ________
Other possible expenses	$ - ________
Balance	$________

Remaining balance is how much money you will have left over after paying all your bills and expenses. (You *will* need to save the one-twelfth of transportation fee money. If you have quarterly and yearly expenses that are not due yet, that will have to be paid later.)

Side note: This doesn't include any luxuries at all—no going to grab something to eat, no movies, no clothes, or any extras.

Luxuries

Any money you have left over will provide you with whatever luxuries you choose to give yourself. It's a good idea to put a few dollars in a savings account every time you get paid even if it is just $10.00, if you can afford it.

There is still more to this moving-out stuff.

Now that you will have your own place, here is what you get to do for yourself:

- earn your own money
- shop and pay for your own groceries
- pay your own house bills
- pay for your cell phone
- pay for your iPad or tablet service bills
- pay for your own auto expenses, registration, gas, and insurance
- possibly pay for your own medical insurance
- possibly pay for your own dental insurance
- pay for other little extras you don't notice
- buy your own clothes
- wash your own clothes
- clean your own place
- take care of yourself when you are sick
- cook for yourself
- get out of bed on time so you are not late for work (if you have a job or are looking for one)

I am sure there will be other stuff you will need. You will figure that out as you go along and realize you don't have it.

Remember, what you *need* and what you *want* are entirely different things now.

All the things you have at home while living with your parents, right now, cost money you didn't have to earn; everything was paid for with your parents' money. These things have been there for you to use and enjoy. You have never missed any of these things because you have had them at your fingertips all along.

For example: You never think about grocery shopping. There is always food in the refrigerator and cupboards. I am sure you didn't go out to buy it with your money, but it is there for you. Same thing with everything that you have been living with at home. It is just there to be used by you.

For you to purchase things for your new home will cost money. It doesn't matter if you buy them from an ad online, at a local store, a yard sale, a secondhand store, or from a friend. You will have to fork out some cash to have the things you need and want.

What other things should you consider?

If your parents pay for most of your expenses because you live at home, they may decide that *since you are moving out, you can pay them yourself, or they may help you with some of them to get you started.* What can some of those things be?

How about any, all, or some of these:

Vehicle Payment

If you have a car to drive and if it's in their name, it is theirs and they can take it and do whatever they want with it or they may let you take it, (if it is paid for), but you have to transfer the title to your name at the motor vehicles department in your state. (There is a fee to do this). You may need proof of auto insurance when you make this transfer. You will need to pay for auto insurance in your name or you may not be able to register your vehicle. If you are lucky enough to keep the vehicle and are transferring it to your name, you can update your license while you are there, with the new address where you will live. Your parents will no longer have to pay another car payment, car insurance, maintenance, car registration, or gas!

Cell Phone

They can take your cell phone and if you refuse to give it to them, they can just cancel your number from their plan. You will need to go to the cell phone service location of your choice and get new service in your name. There may be a fee attached to this too. Since all plans cost different amounts, you may want to review what is within your new budget and your financial obligations. Most parents will let you take the cell phone you have and continue to pay the bill for you under their cell phone agreement.

Laptop, iPad, or Tablet Bill

You may have a laptop or tablet that your parents bought for you to use, and it may have internet access that is paid for by a plan connected with the cell phone bill. Even if your parents will let you take them, if there is a bill attached, they may stop paying that bill. This will now be your responsibility.

Medical Insurance

Do you have any idea how much medical insurance costs? And yes, your parents may have you on their medical insurance plan through their employer. They, most likely, have been paying extra to have you on their insurance and pay a deductible every time you visit the doctor or get medications. By the way, when you turn eighteen, they can legally remove you from their medical insurance because you are an adult, and you are now responsible for your own medical bills and expenses. Many parents may choose to keep their young adults on their medical insurance.

Dental Insurance

Parents or guardians may pay monthly to have dental insurance for the family through their employment's dental insurance policy or some other form of dental insurance. They, most likely, pay a deductible every time you visit the dentist for a cleaning or if you need treatment. By the way, when you turn eighteen, they can legally remove you from their dental insurance because you are an adult, and you are now responsible for your own dental bills and expenses. Many parents may choose to keep their young adults on their dental insurance.

Household Bills

All of you get to enjoy electricity, water, flushing the toilet (sewer), cable, internet, air-conditioning, heat, maybe a yard, and certainly a roof over the house you all live in together. All in all, they will continue to enjoy these amenities without you. Right now, since you live there, you enjoy them too. However, after you move out, you will pay for all these things for your new place with your own money.

Vacations

Your parents may have taken you on family vacations or to visit friends and family that live far from where you live. Now you will all have to discuss if and how this can continue.

Meals Out

Your parents may invite you out to dinner. If they do, be grateful, and accept. Maybe having dinner together every now and then will bring you all closer together, especially if you are on a tight budget and can't afford too many meals out anymore.

Extra Cash

You can ask your parents if you need a few bucks. Depending on your attitude when you ask, they may feel generous and give it to you. *Pay more attention to what they pay for and what it costs because it will likely become one of your new expenses.

Filing Taxes

Every January or February, you will get a W2 form from your employer. You will need this form to file state and federal taxes. But first, talk to your parents about filing taxes. Parents may continue to claim their young adults on their taxes and receive a tax credit for having them as a dependent. Check with your parents before you file your taxes.

What about asking for whatever else you may need?

Demanding anything will certainly not work in your favor nor will threatening never to see them or telling them what horrible parents they are by letting you suffer, never calling them, or trying to guilt trip them.

You attract more ants with sugar. Be nice, be polite, and show some gratitude and respect.

Well, how is it looking for you so far?

Answer a Few Questions for Yourself

Now that I have done the math, can I afford to live on my own without relying on my parents?
Yes__________________________ No____________________________
Are my parents willing to help me financially? Yes ______ No ______
If not, what things can I do differently to get myself financially ready?

____

____

____

____

I have a job. Do I earn enough money? Yes _____ No______
Do I need a second job? Yes _____ No______
Do I need to stop buying things? Yes _____ No______
I don't have a job yet. Do I want to get a job? Yes _____ No______
Am I still too far-off financially to do this? Yes _____ No______

If you are in good financial standing, when you have a place to go, take your clothes and whatever your parents will allow you to take. (Ask for everything in your bedroom. Don't be offended if they say no because your bedroom may become the new guest room, sewing room, office, crafting room, or something else they may like it to be. If they let you take things from your bedroom, it will save you money. Don't forget to thank them!

9

Looking for and Qualifying for a New Home

Look around and see where you would like to live. Go in and ask what their qualifications are and what ages they will accept. Find out if you would even be considered as a tenant.

Do your homework in advance so you know who will let you rent once you are ready. Check out several rental and lease options. Find out what the required monthly rents are and how much the deposit is to move in.

Ask how long will they expect for you to be a tenant. Ask when rent is due and what is included in your rent, i.e., what do they pay for? Do they pay for water, sewer, garbage pickup, cable, etc? Look at your lease *carefully*. Once you sign it, you are committed and married to that house, apartment, or condo for the amount of time it says in writing. Invite your parents to come with you and review the lease before you sign it.

Between the ages of eighteen and twenty-four, or sometimes older, you may have very little credit, if you have any at all. Most rental companies and landlords want to see a minimum one year of employment and income history to satisfy themselves that you can afford to pay the monthly rent in addition to having a good credit score.

They will also want personal references, someone to recommend you and give you some credibility. They may ask for past rental landlord information. If you have never lived away from home, you will not have this. Be honest; tell them you are just starting out and would like to be considered and given the opportunity to prove yourself. (Don't be surprised if they ask if your parents are willing to help by being on your lease as cosigners. This means that if you do not pay the rent, they will contact your parents, and they are just as responsible as you are for the rent and condition you leave the place in when you move out).

When you start working, preferably the year before you move out, talk to your parents or seek out the best way to establish credit, or you may run into walls everywhere you go. Very few people will allow you to rent because of your lack of credit, employment, age, or all those things combined.

Possible Rental or Lease Documentation Requirements

This is a critical point if you are serious about moving out.

Everywhere, you fill out applications regardless of what kind of application it is or what it is for. The company reviewing it may also require some form of documentation.

For rentals and leases:

- Rental Application fees vary depending on the company ($15–$100)
- Driver's License or Identification Card with photo
- Social Security card
- Pay Stubs, two most current
- Bank Statements, two most current

If more than one adult, eighteen years or older will be living in the home with you, the landlord may require a separate application for that person in addition to paying an additional application processing fee. (See sample rental application and sample lease).

Rental Application Sample

Rental property address: ______________________________
Name of applicant: ______________________________
Are you eighteen years of age or over? Yes _____ No _____
Social Security no.: ______________________________
Driver's license no.: __________________ State: ______________
Cell phone: ______________________ Work phone: ___________
Have you ever been convicted of any crime? Yes ____ No ____ If yes, explain on back of application
Present address: ______________________________
How long at this address? _______ Current rental amount: $_______
Reason for moving: ______________________________
Landlord: ___________________ Phone: ______________
Previous address: ______________________________
How long at this address? ________ Current rental amount: $______
Reason for moving: ______________________________
Landlord: ___________________ Phone: ______________
Name, relationship, and ages of all proposed occupants:

____

____

____

____

Waterbed? Yes ______ No ______ Any pets? _____ Describe: _____
Do you or any of the prospective occupants smoke? Yes ___ No ____
Current employer: ______________ Phone: ______________
How long with this employer? ______ Net monthly income: ______
Supervisor: ______________________________
Phone: ______________________________
Previous employer: ______________ Phone: ______________
How long with this employer? _____ Net monthly income: _______
Supervisor: ______________________________
Phone: ______________________________
Other sources of income: ______________________________
Bank name: _________ Branch: ____________ City: ___________
Checking acct no.: ______________ Savings acct no.: ____________

Automobile license plate number: ____________ Make: ___________
Model: ____ Year: ______ Color: _____ State Registered: _________
Personal references: (please do not use family members)
Name: _________________________ Address: _____________________
Phone __________ Relationship: __________ Years acquainted: ____
Name: _________________________ Address: _____________________
Phone __________ Relationship: __________ Years acquainted: ____

I declare that the statements above are true and correct. I hereby give authorization to landlord or landlord's agent to verify all information provided in this application. Permission is granted to interview current and previous landlords and employers, to check criminal record, court records, income, bank account, and credit information. I understand that providing false, misleading, or incomplete information will result in my application being denied.

Applicant signature _____________________ Date _________________
Applicant signature _____________________ Date _________________

Proof of Income

To qualify for a place to live and anything else you may ever want to get on credit, you have to be able to prove you have income. Proof of income comes in a lot of different ways, but typically, whoever is analyzing your qualifications may ask for the last two pay stubs from your job and your last two to three months of bank statements from your checking and savings accounts. Sometimes, you may be asked to provide your current or last two years of Federal Tax Returns. They will certainly ask for a driver's license, passport, or some form of legal identification with a picture of you on it. Once in a while, they ask for your social security card. (They are not allowed to photocopy your social security card).

Rent Payments/Evictions/Credit Reporting and Consequences

Remember, you are an adult, and if you don't pay the rent on time you may be evicted. This translates into breaking a lease. You can be evicted then sued for payment of the remaining time of the lease, court costs, and damages, if any. Landlords may also report this to the credit-reporting agencies where it may stay on your report for many, many years, preventing you from being able to be accepted by other landlords in the future and making it difficult to find another place to live. This may also be a reason you may have to pay higher rents in the future. You will now be seen as a liability as a renter that is very likely to pay rents late, not at all, or are a future eviction risk.

A standard lease requires a twelve-month commitment. Sometimes you may find a place with a six month lease or even a month to month lease. Beware of month to month leases. These leases are openings for landlords to get you in and after a month or two, with a 30 day notice, they can increase your rent. Landlords have the right to increase rents with proper notice as leases expire and are up for renewal. Landlords also have the option of not renewing your lease and asking you to vacate the property or to change the status to a month to month rental. As a rental tenant, if you paid your rents on time during your tenancy, you may request a letter of reference regarding your tenancy and rental payment history which you may use in the future when you move to a new place. A landlord tenant recommendation will help you in the future, and you can use it as a testimony of your good standing and payment history. Ask your landlord to add pertinent information like dates you lived there, how much your rent was every month, the condition you left the place in, and if they would rent to you again. These are the same questions new landlords will ask, and you can hand them a letter answering these questions.

Renting a Room or Getting a Roommate

Renting a room in someone's house may seem ideal (cheaper than a house or apartment). A room in someone's house will be like dating. Everyone will be nice until each finds things about the other that they don't like. This can cause heavy tension in the house, especially if you are sharing common space like the kitchen, bathroom, and living room.

When you are renting and living in an apartment with a roommate, this requires good communication, with all roommates remembering that they are their own housekeepers and cooks. Otherwise, you may end up living in a dirty, trashy, smelly home and will always be arguing. Pick your roommates carefully. You will have to live together. (Roommates should be on your rental or lease agreement so each person shares the legal responsibility and liability).

Apartment Lease Sample

Apartment lease: agreement to lease an unfurnished apartment

By this agreement, made, and entered into on _________ [date], between _________, referred to as "lessor," and _________, referred to as "lessee," lessor demises and lets to lessee, and lessee hires and takes as tenant of lessor, apartment no. _________ of the building _________ [known as _________], situated at (full address) ___ _________ [state], _____ zip _________ to be used and occupied by lessee as residence and for no other use or purpose whatever, for a term of _________ years beginning on _________ [date], and ending on _________ [date], at a rental rate of $_________ per month, payable monthly, in advance, during the entire term of this lease, to lessor at [address] ____ [city], _________ [state], _______ zip _________or to any other person or agent and at any other time or place that lessor may designate.

It is further mutually agreed between the parties as follows:

Security Deposit

On the execution of this lease, lessee deposits with lessor $_________, receipt of which is acknowledged by lessor, as security for the faithful performance by lessee of the terms of this lease agreement, to be returned to lessee, without interest, on the full and faithful performance by lessee of the provisions of this lease agreement.

Number of Occupants

Lessee agrees that leased apartment shall be occupied by no more than _________ [number] persons, consisting of _________ [number] adults and _________ [number] children under the age of _________ years without the prior, expressed, and written consent of lessor.

Assignment and Subletting

Without the prior, expressed, and written consent of lessor, lessee shall not assign this lease, or sublet the premises or any part of the premises. A consent by lessor to one assignment or subletting shall not be deemed to be a consent to any subsequent assignment or subletting.

Showing Apartment for Rental

Lessee grants permission to lessor to show the apartment to new rental applicants at reasonable hours of the day within ____ days of the expiration of the term of this lease.

Entry for Inspection, Repairs, and Alterations

Lessor shall have the right to enter the leased premises for inspection at all reasonable hours and whenever necessary to make repairs and alterations of the apartment or the apartment building or to clean the apartment.

Utilities

Electricity, gas, telephone service, and other utilities are not furnished as a part of this lease unless otherwise indicated in this lease agreement. These expenses are the responsibility of and shall be obtained at the expense of lessee. Charges for _________ [water and garbage service or as the case may be] furnished to the apartment are included as a part of this lease and shall be borne by lessor.

Section 7: Repairs, Redecoration, or Alterations

Lessor shall be responsible for repairs to the interior and exterior of the building, provided, however, repairs required through damage caused by lessee shall be charged to lessee as additional rent. It is agreed that lessee will not make or permit to be made any alterations, additions, improvements, or changes in the leased apartment without in each case first obtaining the written consent of lessor. A consent to a particular alteration/addition, improvement, or change shall not be deemed a consent to or a waiver of restrictions against alterations, additions, improvements, or changes for the future. All alterations, changes, and improvements built, constructed, or placed in the leased apartment by lessee, with the exception of fixtures removable without damage to the apartment and movable personal property, shall, unless otherwise provided by written agreement between lessor and lessee, be the property of lessor and remain in the leased apartment at the expiration or earlier termination of this lease.

Animals

Lessee shall keep no domestic or other animals in or about the apartment or on the apartment house premises without the prior, express, and written consent of lessor.

Waste, Nuisance, or Unlawful Use

Lessee agrees that __________ [he or she] will not commit waste on the premises or maintain or permit to be maintained a nuisance on the premises or use or permit the premises to be used in an unlawful manner.

Waivers

A waiver by lessor of a breach of any covenant or duty of lessee under this lease is not a waiver of a breach of any other covenant or duty of lessee or of any subsequent breach of the same covenant or duty.

Lessee's Holding Over

Parties agree that any holding over by lessee under this lease, without lessor's written consent, shall be a tenancy at will which may be terminated by lessor on _________ days' notice in writing.

Parking Space

Lessee is granted a permit to use parking space no. _________ in the apartment building for the purpose of parking one motor vehicle during the term of this lease.

Option to Review

Lessee is granted the option of renewing this lease for an additional term of _____ [number]______ [months or years] on the same terms and conditions as contained in this lease agreement and at the _________ [monthly or annual] rent of $_________. If lessee elects to exercise this option, _________ [he or she] must give at least _________ days' written notice to lessor prior to the termination of this lease.

Redelivery of Premises

At end of the term of this lease, lessee shall quit and deliver the premises to lessor in good condition with ordinary wear, decay, and damage by the elements excepted.

Default

If lessee defaults payment of rent or any part of rent at times specified above or if lessee defaults in performance of/or compliance with any other term or condition of lease agreement ____ [or of regulations attached to and made a part of lease agreement, which regulations shall be subject to occasional amendment or addition by lessor], the lease, at the option of lessor, shall terminate and be forfeited, and lessor may reenter the premises and retake possession and recover damages, including costs and attorney fees. Lessee shall be given ______ [written] notice of any default or breach. Termination and forfeiture of the lease shall not result if, within ____ days of receipt of such notice, lessee has corrected the default or breach or has taken action reasonably likely to affect correction within a reasonable time.

Destruction of Premises and Eminent Domain

In the event the leased premises are destroyed or rendered useless by fire, storm, earthquake, or other casualty not caused by the negligence of lessee, or if the leased premises are taken by eminent domain, this lease shall be at an end from such time except for the purpose of enforcing rights that may have then accrued under this lease agreement. The rental shall then be accounted for between lessor and lessee up to the time of such injury or destruction or taking of the premises, lessee paying up to such date and lessor refunding the rent collected beyond such date. Should a part only of the leased premises be destroyed or rendered useless by fire, storm, earthquake, or other casualty not caused by the negligence of lessee, the rental shall abate in the proportion that the injured part bears to the whole leased premises. The part so injured shall be restored by lessor as speedily as practicable, after which the full rent shall recommence and the lease continue according to its terms. Any condemnation award concerning the leased premises shall belong exclusively to lessor.

Delay in or Impossibility of Delivery of Possession

In the event possession cannot be delivered to lessee on commencement of the lease term, through no fault of lessor or lessor's agents, there shall be no liability on lessor or lessor's agents, but the rental provided in this lease agreement shall abate until possession is given. Lessor or lessor's agents shall have _________ days in which to give possession, and if possession is tendered within that time, lessee agrees to accept the leased premises and pay the rental provided in this lease agreement. In the event possession cannot be delivered within that time, through no fault of lessor or lessor's agents, then this lease and all rights under this lease agreement shall be at an end.

Binding Effect

The covenants and conditions contained in this lease agreement shall apply to and bind the heirs, legal representatives, and assigns of the parties to this lease agreement, and all covenants are to be construed as conditions of this lease.

Governing Law

It is agreed that this lease agreement shall be governed by, construed, and enforced in accordance with the laws of _________ [state].

Attorney Fees

In the event that any action is filed in relation to this lease agreement, the unsuccessful party in the action shall pay to the successful party, in addition to all the sums that either party may be called on to pay, a reasonable sum for the successful party's attorney fees.

Time of the Essence

It is specifically declared and agreed that time is of the essence of this lease agreement.

Paragraph Headings

The titles to the paragraphs of this lease agreement are solely for the convenience of the parties and shall not be used to explain, modify, simplify, or aid in the interpretation of the provisions of this lease agreement.

In witness, each party to this lease agreement has caused it to be executed at ______________________________ [place of signing] on the date indicated below.

Signature of Lessee __________________________ Date____________

Signature of Lessee __________________________ Date____________

Signature of Lessee __________________________ Date____________

10

Landlord Expectations

You Have a Place to Live

Before moving in, I suggest you take a camera and a piece of paper and go over the house inch by inch, taking photos of anything that may be damaged, worn, or a concern to you. Write everything down and make copies of all the damages. Write a letter to the landlord—you and a witness should sign it—make a copy for yourself, attach it to the copies of the photographs of damages you see, and mail to the landlord. If you don't do this, you may end up paying for damages that you didn't cause. If the landlord insists on doing the walk-through with you, don't be shy, point things out, and take notes and pictures to protect yourself. Protect yourself or pay.

Whether house or apartment, the landlord will have expectations. The first expectation is that you pay the rent on time. The landlord will also expect that you keep the exterior of the home, yard, and patios neat and clean and that the interior also be well cared for and maintained.

The landlord has a right to give you proper notice, typically between twenty-four and seventy-two hours' notice that he or she is coming to the house and see how it is being cared for inside and out.

The landlord will expect that if *anything* breaks, leaks, or becomes damaged that you report it right away. Maintenance left defective can cause more extensive damages, and you may be responsible for the cost of repair.

Landlords will sometimes drive by to see how things look on the exterior, and more than likely, every neighbor has your landlord's phone number and can call if they have any concerns.

What You Should *Never* Do in Your New Home

Allowing drugs and alcohol into your new home is a good way of getting evicted.

These additional things can also get you an eviction notice:

- Loud disturbances and noise is also a good way of getting evicted.
- Disturbing the neighbors and getting evicted because all your friends are hanging out at your new place, and partying can be very bad.
- Unless you are twenty-one, alcohol is illegal, and drugs are always illegal.
- Providing minors under the age of twenty-one alcohol, drugs, or tobacco is illegal.
- Legal drinking age may vary from state to state. Be aware of what it is in your state.

Once a tenant is evicted, it's almost impossible to find a landlord that will rent to you. Did you know that in many states if you allow someone to spend the night in your home and they refuse to leave, you can't throw them out? Did you know that you have to go through the entire legal process and formally evict them? It is also very expensive.

Keeping all those things in mind, are you ready?

11

Personal Property Item Search

Here are some helpful suggestions that may help you get what you need:

- Go through your parents' garage and look for things you may need that your parents have stored and may be extra. (Ask for permission to take anything you need). Saves you more money.
- Look for pots and pans, dishes, linens, small appliances, etc.
- Go online and look for free things that people are giving away.
- Go to yard and garage sales and bargain for things you need.
- Go to flea markets and bargain for things.
- Go to secondhand stores.
- Post want and need ads on local community websites.
- Ask friends and family for things you may need that they have lying around the garage or in a storage room.

This is real. Take all your things that you no longer need or use, trade them for things you need and maybe you can help yourself by going in this direction. Be resourceful.

Most parents are pretty good; they will keep helping you in a few different ways after you move out. Most help if you are helping yourself and have proven yourself to be responsible.

What else will you have to pay for and what *other* things you are going to need?

What's in your new place and what do you have to buy? Use this handy checklist to figure it out:

- microwave
- stove
- refrigerator
- coffeepot
- toaster
- dishwasher
- magic bullet or blender
- pots
- pans
- baking dishes
- spoons, forks, and knives
- cooking and serving utensils
- serving dishes
- measuring cups and measuring spoons
- plates, bowls, cups, and glasses
- kitchen towels
- dining room table and chairs
- television set
- sofa and love seat
- comfy chair
- maybe a coffee table and end tables
- curtains, drapes, or blinds throughout the place
- wall hangings to make your place feel like home

For your bedroom, you may need the following:

- bed with frame, box spring, and mattress
- sheets
- blankets
- pillows
- dresser
- nightstand
- lamps
- mirror
- laundry basket

If you have a yard, patio or porch, you might want the following:

- outdoor furniture
- barbecue grill or hibachi

Garage:

If you are lucky enough to have a garage, you can use it to store some of your other stuff, and if you have a car, park it inside. (You're an adult now and you are responsible for all your material things; *take them with you*).

If you do not you have room for everything in your new place, what are you doing with the rest of that stuff? Sell it? Donate it? Take it to the dump? You can't leave it at your parents' house, and you shouldn't.

Auto Maintenance—Things everyone should know

As previously discussed, a vehicle is the responsibility of the owner.

Many people do know about mechanical things that involve vehicles.

For those who don't, these are a few things you NEED TO KNOW.

Members of Roadside Assistance Clubs can just call the 800 number and get help to come to them at just about any location. But what happens when you are not in a serviceable area or you're not a member of one of those services?

Know some very needed information about your vehicle that is basic.

For example, everyone should know these basics:

KNOW HOW TO READ YOUR DASHBOARD AND WHAT THINGS MEAN WHEN THEY LIGHT UP!!!

- Check how much fuel your vehicle has every day.
- Know where on your vehicle you refill the fuel.
- Know what kind of fuel is recommended for your vehicle.
- Know what type of oil your car uses.
- Know how and where to check the oil. (Without enough oil, you can blow out the engine and end up without a vehicle)
- Know how and where to add oil to the vehicle and how much.
- Know how and where to check the transmission oil.
- Know how and where to add transmission oil and how much.
- Know how and where to check the coolant.
- Know how and where to add coolant and how much.
- Know how and where to check the window washing fluid.
- Know how and where to add window washing fluid and how much.
- Where is the spare tire and is it in serviceable condition?
- Are the tools in the vehicle in case you have to change a tire?

- Is there a can of "Flat Repair" in your vehicle that may be useful to get you to a service station to repair shop? If not, get one and know how to use it.
- Know how to change a tire correctly.

I recommend that in the trunk of every vehicle a milk crate type box be kept with the following items:

- Container of coolant
- Quart of oil
- Quart of transmission oil
- Funnels for oil
- Can of Flat Repair
- Rags to check fluids
- Jumper cables and tools to change a tire.

Make it a habit to check the fluids once every two weeks or every time you fill up your tank.

Service your vehicle as recommended. Some are every three thousand miles, some are every five thousand miles. Know what the recommendation is for your vehicle.

Regularly check:

- Front lights
- Tail lights
- Turn signal lights
- Fog lights
- High beams
- Wear and tear of tires. (Have regularly scheduled tire rotations and brake checks for safety).

Most important of all, this note:

DO NOT DRINK AND DRIVE

DO NOT TEXT AND DRIVE – All states are cell phone "hands free" states and DO NOT allow texting while driving,

WEAR A SEAT BELT AND HAVE ALL PASSENGERS WEAR SEATBELTS

DOGS CAN WEAR SAFETY BELTS TOO AND SHOULD.

Fines are ENORMOUS if you get a citation for any of the above violations.

Driving under the influence and causing any accident can bring on consequences that can't even be imagined and possibly cause death of the driver, passengers or people outside of any vehicle. (Just watch the news and learn more).

Being pulled over intoxicated can ruin so many things it will make anyone's head spin, and depending on the incident, can cause the vehicle to be impounded. (Get a load of what it will cost to get the vehicle back)!

Every accident that now occurs is investigated to determine if the driver was texting and driving or on a cell phone call. The discovery determines the charges. Even if the accident is caused by someone else, both parties are investigated for texting or being distracted by a cell phone call.

Seatbelts are the law in every state. Simply put—WEAR A SEAT BELT and make sure everyone in the vehicle you are driving wears one as well. The driver of every vehicle is responsible for their passengers wearing seatbelts.

Any driver may be stopped and cited for not wearing a seatbelt or for the passengers not wearing seatbelts, regardless that no other laws are being broken.

For example:

While in a vehicle, if it is in drive position and a text is being sent or a phone is being answered using hands, it is illegal.

Even if the light is red and you are stopped waiting for it to change. To legally send texts or make calls using hands, the vehicle must be off the road and the engine must be turned off.

Weapons in vehicles:

In most states it is illegal to have a weapon in a vehicle. Know the laws in your state about weapons in vehicles. It could be a life or death choice.

12

Real-Life Experiences

Mark G.

I really wanted to move out. I don't think I was a bad guy when I lived at home. I didn't like doing the house jobs my parents gave me, but I did them. I didn't stay out too late or get into trouble. I did have a few beers here and there with my friends, and I did smoke. My parents didn't know I drank, but they knew I smoked, and they really didn't like that. Most of the time, that is what we fought about.

I told my parents I wanted to move out after I graduated. They told me how hard it would be and that I had to earn and budget my money to be able to make it. They also told me that if I went to school full-time, I could keep living at home and they would pay for everything. I really wanted to be on my own. I wanted to move out.

During the summer before my senior year, I got a job at a fast-food place not too far from my house. I rode my bike to and from work every day. I asked for extra shifts because I wanted more money to move. My parents were surprised at the focus I had to do this. My grades were still fine, so everything was going pretty well. After my senior year, I kept working at the fast-food place, and I enrolled at a local community college. It was too far for me to ride my bike to the college, so my parents bought me monthly bus passes. Finally, I thought it was time for me to move. I had enough money saved. I started looking at studio apartments and they were too expensive, and no one would take an application from me. I ended up looking online at rooms for rent. That was all my budget could afford.

I looked at lots of rooms. People wouldn't give me a chance because I was only eighteen, and they thought I would bring all of my friends to hang out there. I had to do something different. I decided to call first. I would tell them my story that I had a job and I was a student. I hoped that would help. I tried to make them like me before they met me so I wouldn't waste my time and go there for nothing.

It felt weird to be in people's houses looking at rooms. I found a furnished room that came with a bed, nightstands, dresser, bathroom with shower, and had its own entrance that didn't go through the house. I liked that one the best. I liked that no one would know when I was coming in or leaving, and it felt like a studio. It was perfect. I would have more privacy. I also had use of the kitchen and laundry room, but since I didn't cook and I ate at work, I was okay with it. I would just get a microwave and small refrigerator. I brought my parents to see it and to meet the guy and his wife. My parents thanked them for giving me a chance by renting to me. (They think I didn't see them give my new landlords their phone number, but I saw that). At $700 a month, it included house bills and Wi-Fi access. Sounded good to me. I signed a six-month lease and handed the guy a cashier's check for $1,400. That was my deposit and the first month of rent. I was very excited. I packed my stuff at home, and my parents helped me move in. I packed all my extra stuff in boxes and put them in a corner of my parents' garage for safekeeping.

Everything was going well for about eight months. I had to cut my hours at work because I had so much homework for my classes; I wasn't earning enough money. I couldn't afford anything extra, and now, I couldn't afford my rent. I had used up most of my savings making up to pay the rent. Since I didn't renew my lease and it turned into a month-to-month rental, I gave my thirty-day notice and moved back home after talking to my parents. The guy was really nice and let me use my deposit to pay my last month's rent as long as I cleaned the room really good and it was ready for a new renter. I didn't want to work so much that I couldn't go to school. I wanted to have a good job so I could have things I wanted. Working in a fast-food restaurant forever was not part of my plan.

Steve M.

After high school, I moved in with my buddies. Four of us lived in the house. It was easy because my friend's parents owned the house. I didn't have to have a credit report or much of a deposit. I had a job, and my rent was cheap—$300 and one-fourth of the house bills.

No one took care of the cleaning or the yard, and pretty soon, the house was always trashed. My mom and dad were great when I went home even though they knew why I was there. I would go home to do my laundry because I didn't have laundry soap, and they would invite me to stay for dinner. All our friends spent their time at our place. They all ate what food was in the house, but none of them helped pay for any of it. We all partied all the time, and we worked when we had to. My friend's parents usually called before they came over, and we'd all hurry up and clean up the house and the yard. The neighbors started calling them because we had lots of parties and cars. Sometimes, it got a little loud, and finally, the neighbors stopped coming to bang on the door and just called the police and my friend's parents. The last time, they all showed up at the same time. It was a mess. Some of the guys were not legal to drink, and the police called their parents to come and get them. Bottom line, we all got evicted from the house, and they used our deposits to clean it all up so they could find new renters. My friend's parents told us not to use them as a landlord reference. Nothing was worse than the lecture I got when I had to move back into my parents' house and hearing how disappointed they were and that they knew I would do something like this.

Eventually, I will be able to move out on my own, but next time, I won't be sharing a house with anyone. Even though my rent was cheap, I still kept running out of money and having to ask for loans from my friends and my parents. Since I don't want to go to college, I just get jobs doing things I like to do. I am saving money again to try to move out.

Grace H.

How did my move out go? It went very badly. I had been out of high school for two years when I moved out. (I didn't want to go to school anymore and decided not to go to college). I got a job at a retail store as a shelf stocker. The pay wasn't that great, but I was hoping to work my way up and hoping it wouldn't take too long to be a supervisor and make more money. I had to work weekends and couldn't hang out with my friends too much because I was tired, and on my days off, they were in school or working too. I had been working at the store for one year when I met my boyfriend. We became inseparable. At the beginning of my second year at my job, he asked me if I wanted us to get a place together. I was really excited and said yes. We both saved our money, and when we had enough, we rented a one-bedroom apartment. We couldn't afford very much, so we asked our parents if we could have things that were in their garages and got stuff from aunts and uncles and from people that didn't want their things anymore, like our bed, dishes, mismatched coffeepot, and pictures for the walls. We had lived there for four months when I found out I was pregnant. I freaked out and could not stop crying because my boyfriend and I were not getting along very well. I was scared to tell him, and I was scared to tell my mom and dad. I told him first, and he was really upset and said he thought I was using birth control. The truth is, I was, and then one day, I forgot and just stopped taking my pills. He said he wasn't ready because he still had a lot of things he wanted to do. I didn't have big plans yet, but I knew having a baby wasn't part of my plan either. He moved out.

Now I was alone, scared, pregnant, and had a job that didn't pay enough to afford the rent. I called my parents. They were really, really upset. My dad suggested an abortion or that I have the baby and give it to his parents. My dad suggested adoption, and then he said I would have to find a place I could afford with what I earn, and if I chose to keep the baby that I should ask the baby's father for child support because I was going to need it. I couldn't go back home. My parents would not allow me to move back because I was pregnant, and they said, "You and that baby's daddy should work together and figure this thing out." I applied for welfare, food stamps, and had to go to the Red Cross for help when I got the eviction notice taped to my front door.

I was almost twenty, and my life felt like it was a disaster.

What was I supposed to do with this baby? Ex-boyfriend was long gone.

I went to a church and talked to the pastor. He sent me to talk to someone else, and after three or four someone else's, they found me a room at a girls' home where other young mothers also lived. I visited my parents on weekends, and I spent the night sometimes, but it was never the same. I felt like I was not welcomed and that they allowed this out of obligation. All my friends slowly disappeared because I couldn't go out and party and hang out anymore. Once the baby was born, I fell in love and could not give her up. (That was my plan, to keep my baby). Now I am a single mom. I love my baby with all my heart and would never do anything to hurt her. I live with another single mom, and we take turns watching each other's baby so each of us can go to work and know our babies are safe. I see my parents when I can, and sometimes, they even offer to babysit. I still get government assistance for medical needs, WIC, and food stamps. Still no child support, and the ex has still not seen his baby.

Getting pregnant changed my life. I wasn't even old enough to drink, and now, I am raising a baby all by myself. I am very grateful to have a good roommate that understands exactly what I am going through. She and I are doing this together.

Side note: These are just a few people that shared their experiences. I am sure if I stopped young people and asked them their stories, I could fill a book with what went right, what went wrong, what they would do differently, and how they are surviving today.

Think about the consequences of each decision before you make it. Those decisions can be your life's game changer.

Date Rape and Safety Tips

Ladies, this topic is most common for you. The expectation is that male companions protect you, however, sometimes your date is the bad guy.

Before jumping into that dating landmine, do your homework about him. Who are his friends, associates, where does he work, is he responsible, honest, and is he respected. Look around and ask about his reputation, ask questions, make yourself aware. Look him up on social media.

Who else has he dated?
Why did it end?
Was it amicable?
How does he talk about his former girlfriends?
What about his friends? What are they like?

Don't go to his place. Be careful of the "I forgot something at my place, do you mind if we stop there on our way."

Be aware of your surroundings, try to double date when you don't know the person and go to public places.

Going out with someone new? Send their name, phone number and photo and if possible, car license number to friends and family. Tell them where you are going and guestimate a time you plan on being back home. Call or text the people you send this information to so they know you are safely home.

Let him know you are doing this and that you do this to be safe.

Let your date know you are sending his name, photo, phone number, what kind of car and color with license plate number to your friends and family. Say that you do this for your safety and so people know who you are with.

ANYPLACE YOU GO, NEVER LEAVE YOUR DRINKS OUT OF YOUR SIGHT, EVER!

If you are offered a drink and someone is "going to get it for you," GO WITH THEM! Again, do not drink anything you are given that has not been in your sight from the minute a can or bottle is opened or a cocktail is poured.

Learn more about date rape drugs and how they are used on innocent people.

It is more critical today to do all of this to be safe. It is always recommended that all people take self defense classes. I strongly recommend this as well.

Safety is first. If you are not practicing safety, it may cost you emotional trauma and distress for many years, or it may cost you your life.

All genders of people are susceptible to date rape, some may not believe they can be at risk of date rape drugs, but they can. If at any time you feel you have been a victim of date rape, do not hesitate to contact authorities. It is a sexual crime. It should be reported no matter who the person was that you believe committed this sexual crime against you.

Sexual Harassment

Everyone has heard of sexual harassment. It seems to be in the headline news, on TV and the internet everyday.

Know what it really is and what is considered sexual harassment. Companies now have training classes on identifying sexual harassment, what it is and why it should be stopped. Sexual harassment is being reported to employers and employees are warned not to participate in this behavior. Here are a few situations considered sexual harassment that can happen, be seen and heard by anyone in the workplace, not just subordinates, but by business owners, employers and supervisors as well:

- talking about sex openly in the work place
- making sexual comments
- making sexual gestures
- touching someone inappropriately
- sexually propositioning someone
- cornering someone in a sexually uncomfortable manner
- continuously being in someone's personal space that doesn't want you there
- your job being threatened if you do not perform sexual favors
- supervisors asking for sexual favors in exchange for promotions
- employees offering sex in return for favors or promotions

There are more lawsuits every day by people suing for sexual harassment and creating a hostile environment in the workplace. If you are a victim of sexual harassment, follow the company protocol for reporting these incidents and keep a log of everything that happens, dates, times, who you report it to, what is being done to stop it and make sure to keep checking in to find out how it is being resolved without ending up in court suing your employer for not doing anything about the harassment.

Be aware, protect yourself, steer clear of anyone that you see doing any of these things and report any incidents immediately.

13

Some Game Changers

Surprise! Lots of things can go wrong. Some of them will be within your control and others will not. They will be bumps in your road. You will need to make adjustments accordingly to make things work. Some will be easier than others and they will keep coming.

Out of your control would be things like:

- losing a job (unless it is your fault due to irresponsibility)
- hours cut at work
- getting sick
- losing a roommate that helped pay bills
- and a list of other unforeseen things

And there is this, one of the *huge* ones you *can control* and you should control.

The Pregnancy Game Changer

For every pregnant female, there is a male who got her that way. Statistics will follow. Both males and females will *want* see what the chances are of being a statistic too.

Pregnancy prevention is the responsibility of both people.

Pregnancy game changer for ladies

If you are a female and have moved out, having an unexpected pregnancy *changes everything*—yes, a real game changer for ladies and for all baby daddies, especially if you live alone or live with a roommate and the father lives in his own home and you are dating or living apart.

Side note for the men will follow. For now, here is a side note for ladies: Some baby daddies are keepers, some baby daddies are users, some baby daddies are baby makers that move on to someone else, some baby daddies are drug users, alcoholics, smooth-talking players, physical abusers, verbal abusers, and a long grocery list of other challenging behaviors. Don't get me wrong here, ladies, every one of those behaviors above is the same about many women too. The difference is that chances are *incredibly high that you will be the one raising the child that you are carrying*. Regardless of which kind of baby momma you are from that same list above, that baby is your responsibility for the rest of its life. Rarely does a baby daddy end up with the baby, so that parenting responsibility falls on you. So don't be fooled by men who say it doesn't feel as good with a condom, or I am fixed and can't get you pregnant.

Ladies, always protect yourself from possible pregnancy. Condoms are one of the most effective ways to protect yourself from pregnancy and sexually transmitted diseases, next to abstinence of course. If you become pregnant, you can't come back with "You said you couldn't get me pregnant." It is your responsibility too! Ladies, having a pregnancy is *your game changer*. In addition to being pregnant, you will still have bills, you still have to work, and now you have to do all these while feeling tired, emotional, hormonal, and always hungry. All these and nine months of pregnancy are ahead. Some women are lucky enough to change living situations and baby's father and mother move in together to create a family and do the best they can to make a good home for all of them. This is not easy at such a young age, but it is possible. How long this living situation lasts may vary from a short period to a long term or lifetime loving commitment. This situation will take more time, energy, and work since your financial lives and education are not yet in good, stable order.

Here are a few things to consider:

How long will you be together? This may depend on both of your maturity levels, commitment to each other and commitment to having a family, your attitude, and if this is the life you both were hoping to have that just came sooner than expected. Is this what *he* really wanted? Is this what *you* really wanted?

Pregnancy statistics will follow. Statistics show that a VERY high percentage of women end up raising a child or children without a father. A majority of young women are forced to use government assistance like welfare, food stamps, WIC, women's shelters, free community assistance programs, church assistance programs, Red Cross, and the Salvation Army, just to name a few.

Here are a few other things to consider:

Your friends will change. Friends without kids will move on without you. It doesn't appear that way now, but it will happen. Your new friends will be women in a situation just like yours. Your Friday and Saturday nights will be at home taking care of your baby. Welcome to being an adult and a mother. Your life will never be the same in both good and bad ways. You get to decide what kind of mother you are going to be and you get to start before the baby is born, and it will continue as soon as the baby arrives. Some lucky young women have the support of their parents and baby daddy and live together as a family, and they get help from baby daddy's family. Baby mommas may have to turn to their parents and some are allowed to move back home if things go awry. Many young women, in moving back home, get help from parents in raising the child, paying bills, and helping with childcare. Some parents will not be so supportive in giving this amount of help. Sometimes, the child's father and father's family will participate and help with necessary supplies if they can. Some parents don't have the means, and other parents will pretend you and the child do not exist.

Whether you choose to keep your baby, put your baby up for adoption, or get an abortion, the choice you make is what you will live with for the rest of your life.

Men and pregnancy: Beware of women that try to trap you by getting pregnant or by telling you they are on birth control when they are not. If you are having sex, bring *your own* condoms! Many women are honest; some women are not.

Whether you live with baby momma or not, if you are the baby's daddy, you are part of the new situation. Your money is no longer your own. I say your money because that will be all you will be required to give baby momma, for now. Once the baby is born, you get to divide all the costs to support your new baby. If you are not living with baby momma and baby, you will be supporting the baby financially until the courts tell you differently. You are the baby daddy and your job will be to love, protect, and support the new baby. Some of you will be honorable and do the right thing. Some of you will do all you can, and some of you will behave like irresponsible man-children. Others will abandon a pregnant woman and child as if it isn't your fault or your problem. Guess what? Baby momma has the right the minute that baby is born to file for child support in a court of law. A judge will decide what you will be required to pay her monthly, and as time goes by, the more money you earn, the more money she can ask for. The cost of raising a child is very high. (In 2017, it was announced that to raise a child, the cost is at minimum about $234,000)! Go to the store and look at the cost of diapers, formula, baby food, children's clothing, a crib, swing, car seat, stroller, bottles, and baby food. Things a baby needs are endless just as endless as the needs that will come up until they are old enough for you to stop paying child support. They also need medical and dental insurance!

Oh, and take a minute to look at the cost of day care. If nothing scares you, that will. Did I mention that if you can't pay your child support payments right away, it adds up? That's right, and the minute you get a job and file tax returns, Uncle Sam will claim your tax return and give it to baby momma. Your weekly or biweekly paycheck may be garnished (money taken out to send to baby momma). Unpaid child support accrues interest at a high rate. Unpaid child support is reported to the credit reporting agencies, ruining your credit. If you have a professional license of any kind, it may jeopardize your license, career, ability to get or keep a job, get a place to live and cause so many other problems. Did you know you may be arrested in some states for not paying child support? There are men and some women living below the poverty level just because of not being able to pay child support!

You may not live with that baby, but you *will pay* for that baby for a long time, and it will come from what you will earn from baby's birth until the courts says you are done. If you have any doubts that you are the baby's daddy, you are about to take on eighteen years of paying or supporting a baby. You may petition the courts for a paternity test as verification.

Is It *Not* Clear That This Pregnancy Prevention Is the Responsibility of Both People?

Most young men do not have a steady income or sufficient income for financially helping raise a child. Many people at a young age don't earn enough money to pay child support or for the things a child will need. Therefore, you are both on your own to do what every parent does *sacrifice everything* to take care of a child.

Take a look at the statistics that follow.

Teen Pregnancy Statistics

Even though the teen pregnancy rate has declined over the past few decades, the fact of the matter is that the United States has the highest teen pregnancy rate of the Western industrialized world. It is true that the teen pregnancy and birth rate was much higher prior to 1980 (and especially in the 1950s and 1960s), but at the time, young women were getting married and having children before the age of 20. Most of the teen pregnancies occurring before 1980 were to married women; now most of today's teen mothers are unwed.

See the following interesting teen pregnancy statistics:

- In 2013, 273,105 babies were born to girls ages 15–19.
- In 2013, there were 26.5 births for every 1,000 girls ages 15–19.
- 89% of teenage parents are unmarried.
- Some 86,000 teens aged 15–17 gave birth in 2012.
- Nearly 1,700 teens aged 15–17 give birth every week.
- About 77% of teenage pregnancies are unplanned.
- 4 in 10 teenage girls who had sex at 13 or 14 report the sex was unwanted or involuntary.
- 15% of teen pregnancies end in miscarriage.
- 30% of teenage pregnancies end in abortion.

Teen Pregnancy by Ethnicity in 15–19-Year-Old Girls:

- 41.7 per 1,000 Hispanic girls reported a teen pregnancy in 2013.
- 39.0 per 1,000 black girls reported a teen pregnancy in 2013.
- 18.6 per 1,000 white girls reported a teen pregnancy in 2013.

These teen pregnancy statistics have changed dramatically:

- Hispanic teens consist of approximately 87.3% per 1,000.
- Black teens consist of approximately 79.2% per 1,000.
- White teens consist of approximately 32.6% per 1,000.

What about these teen pregnancy statistics?

- 3 million 15–19-year-old girls have unsafe abortions every year.
- 50% of teen mothers up to age 19 have high school diplomas.
- 80% of unmarried teen mothers end up on welfare.
- 22% of teen mothers have mothers who were also teen mothers.
- Sons of teenage mothers have a 13% chance of ending up in prison.
- 15% of all 15-years-olds have had sex.
- 39% of all 17-year-olds have had sex.
- 72% of sexually active teens want access to birth control.
- 73% of teens that were surveyed believe virginity should not be embarrassing.
- 67% of the teens in the survey wish they would have waited to have sex.

On a worldwide scale:

- 16 million teens give birth each year.
- 49 of every 1,000 girls, globally, give birth.
- 15–19-years-olds have the second highest rate of death due to childbirth.

Besides pregnancy, what else can come from sex without protection that can cause illness and be a huge game changer too?

Look up some of these sexually transmitted diseases that can be shared between men and women. See if they are worth getting because you chose not to use a condom:

HPV	HIV	AIDS	Chlamydia	Genital Warts
Gonorrhea	Hepatitis	Herpes	Syphilis	

- 1 in 4 girls nationwide has a sexually transmitted disease.
- Each year, 1 in 4 teens contracts an STD/STI.
- 1 out of 2 sexually active person will contract an STD/STI by age 25.

Be careful, *a person can have several STDs at the same time*. Some can never be controlled with medication while others can be deadly. Most of them can be shared with a sexual partner. Would someone tell you they have an STD? Would you tell someone if you do? A sexually transmitted disease could be a life-and-death illness, or it could be a new permanent illness. Before starting a new sexual relationship, go get tested at a local clinic together.

Take a look at the websites provided just so you have information on hand that may help if you need it. Visit these eye-opening websites:

- TeenHelp.com
- CDC.gov Preventing Pregnancies in Younger Teens
- who.int "Adolescent Pregnancy" [Online]
- cdc.gov "Preventing Pregnancies in Younger Teens" [Online]
- cdc.gov "About Teen Pregnancy" [Online]
- hhs.gov "Trends in Teen Pregnancy and Childbearing" [Online]
- FamilyFirstAid.org "Teen Pregnancy Statistics and Teen Pregnancy Facts" [Online]
- TheNationalCampaign.org "Fast Facts: Teen Pregnancy in the United States" [Online]

At young ages, *most of the time*, neither of you is old enough or mature enough for the responsibility to parent a child. If you want to try, here are a few things to think about. Look into some things I've shared about your possible life and your possible future. Your life will depend on the choices *you* make. Any consequences will be because of *your* decisions. Choose wisely by considering the consequences first and being prepared!

14

Other Options

Other Employment and Training Options

If you want to just get out and turn yourself into a real adult in training, you do have other options. You have endless options. You just have to look for how to get to the final place of successful employment, living situation, and your own place of peace. If you don't want to rely on your parents anymore, consider researching one or all these possible options to see if, maybe, any one of them is the right fit for you.

To be accepted into a military service, you will need to take a test or two, pass a physical examination and, possibly, a mental evaluation. Once you get past that, you move forward with your enlistment. In any military service, if you have a college degree, you may be accepted to join as an officer at a higher rank and pay scale—something you can work toward if you don't have a degree yet and may be planning on working toward. If you are an enlisted soldier, you have opportunities to work your way up in the ranks. Your efforts are rewarded with added rank and pay raises. All of the services have a period of physical training, a.k.a. boot camp, followed by formal educational training in the field you will have chosen when you enlisted. Once your trainings are completed, you are assigned to serve at the next available place that has an opening for your job type. This could be any place in the U.S. or in the world. Travel is involved; almost every three years you will make a move. By the way, did I mention that the definition of GI is "government issue"? That is correct. Once you sign on, you are the property of the government, agreeing to do all that is asked of you.

Did I also mention that if you join the military at eighteen years old, you can retire by the time you are thirty-eight years old and have income for retirement, medical, and dental insurance forever? And if you get bored, you still have time to find another job you can enjoy and earn a second income. Depending on the job, you can work for the government, doing the same thing or something similar and work toward a second retirement income. Easy street after that. This is why it's important to pick a career that can work inside of the military and outside of the military. If you decide to serve, I'd like to be the first to thank you in advance for your choice to serve in protecting the freedom of the country.

After all of that, if you would consider serving in the military, before signing on the dotted line, think seriously about what kind of job would serve you best. What kind of a job will give you a good, healthy, balanced salary and one you wouldn't mind doing *after* you are released from your service. Consider these types of careers and some along the lines of daily need of the population and that everyone needs at one time or another; these career jobs can provide job security any place in the world. Research potential job incomes in the civilian community before selecting a job in the military that you want to continue to do as a civilian, even if you don't stay in and serve until retirement.

Every job in the civilian job market is also available in the military. Pick your passion.

Just to name a few lines of employment:

- Medical
- Technological
- Electrical
- Computer sciences
- Aviation
- Maintenance
- Administration
- Engineering
- Finance

Look online and find out the criteria for joining any of the military services. *Do not* go there or be pressured into taking a job you don't want. They always try to fill the unwanted positions first and make them sound so good.

When you walk in, have your research complete and have a list of the jobs you want in your hand!

Many military recruiters, not all of them, are like used car salespeople—quick sales line, high pressure, and get you to sign right there on the spot.

Do not be afraid or nervous. They *need you*. Be up front about what you want. Ask if any of those jobs on your list have sign-on bonuses. Tell them you want to know about their branch contribution toward furthering your education.

Do not sign anything that day. Go to all of them and ask the same questions. Tell them you are visiting all the branches to look for the best offer. Shop for your career as if you are shopping for a favorite item. This is your future!

Compare what they are all offering. *Do not* sign anything unless you have someone else look at it first.

Don't fall for the sell lines like:

"This offer is only good for today."

"This is the last position open in this field. You have to sign today to get it."

"Let me see if I can get them to hold that job while you give it some thought." (They walk away and talk to someone else, come back, and say, "No, you have to sign today to secure the last spot.")

"If you really want this job, you have to sign right now. Lots of other people want this job too."

Bottom line is that we have one of the largest military forces in the world, and there are plenty of jobs, none that are not offered at another branch or that will not be there another day.

Take time to *get the job that you want*!

Here is a list of military service branches available to you and their websites:

- www.USArmy.com
- www.USNavy.com
- www.USAirForce.com
- www.USMarines.com
- www.GoCoastGuard.com

Here is a different option: Job Corps (www.JobCorps.gov) is the nation's largest and most comprehensive residential education and job-training program. Job Corps is a free education and training program that helps young people learn a career, earn a high school diploma or GED, and find you a good job. *Free free free free free free!* If you don't want to join the military but want a place to live, medical, dental, vision insurance, meals, an allowance, an education, and training in a job that can keep you employed, this option is free if you are between seventeen and twenty-four years old. It does offer everything you need to start your own life by getting the job certifications you need to have a career. You just need to want to do it.

If you are interested in joining Job Corps or would like more information, all you have to do is call (800) 733-JOBS or (800) 733-5627. This program is offered only in the United States.

15

Resource Guide

If you get to the point of needing help, keep in mind that you should talk to your parents first and family members next. They will be the ones to help you get through the tough times, and they may make suggestions to help and guide you. If that is not an option, use resources available to you. For example, if you are renting a house or apartment and can no longer afford it, consider moving back home or renting a less expensive apartment or room. If parents won't let you move back home, consider asking a family member or family friend.

There are also other resources that can help you with housing and food, places like:

- Red Cross
- Salvation Army
- church and church groups
- homeless shelters and group homes

There are several locations that have food banks and give away food for free. Many community groups and churches also have these services.

If you are a student, talk to your school counselor and ask for help.

These are just a few suggestions. Keep in mind that most people will help someone that is trying to help him or herself.

Young Adults in Foster Care.

What does happens to your life when you turn eighteen?
Where do you go?
What will you do?
Where will you live?
How will you feed yourself?
How will you get clothes you need?
What about medical, dental and other medical needs?
What will you use for transportation?
Who will you go to when you need help?

Lots of tough questions to seriously consider and it will be helpful to have some answers.

Lets get started.

Prior to aging out of a foster program, consider setting up what will be your next move. It would be helpful to make yourself familiar with as many local Foster Youth Advocacy Programs as possible. Most states have programs to assist young adults in many of their cities, and they are there to assist young adults in foster programs to make that transition into new housing. Many would like to see these foster program young adults flourish by continuing their education and fulfilling their goals of having a happy and full life.

Most states have a number of programs that can be found online. I suggest an online search like the examples below:

- Foster Youth Advocacy San Diego California

- Foster Youth Advocacy San Francisco California
- Foster Youth Advocacy Hilo Hawaii
- Foster Youth Advocacy Duluth Minnesota
- Foster Youth Advocacy Las Vegas Nevada
- Foster Youth Advocacy Nashville Tennessee
- Foster Youth Advocacy New York, New York
- Foster Youth Advocacy Charleston South Carolina

You get the picture.

The people in these programs will be able to guide you in the right direction, and you may find a great mentor or mentors within the advocacy program that can be a "go-to" person or people that can serve you as a surrogate family.

They have experience and knowledge of how to help you and get you set up with several services that may help make your road to a new home, school, insurance, transportation and other important things that you may need as you're learning and growing into self sufficiency.

Remember, the foster programs are filled with young people of all ages. Don't let yourself fall in-between the cracks and end up without the support that is out there to help you.

Once it's time to leave your program, it's best to have things lined up to make your move.

Outside of the program you're in, no one knows you need help unless you seek it out and ask for it. People are not mind readers. You have to ask directly for the guidance you need and for recommendations and advice someone may be able to give you.

There is no shame in asking for help and guidance. There is no shame in asking someone to be a mentor and a personal advocate to you. Many people are honored and feel privileged that a young adult would respect them enough to ask them to be a mentor. These people may become new longtime friends.

Don't hold yourself back. Take a deep breath and JUMP! Start getting yourself ready to have the life you deserve with "A Little Help From Some Friends."

Side note to those of you in foster care programs:

REPORT ANY KIND OF ABUSE YOU SEE OR EXPERIENCE WHILE IN A FOSTER HOME.

Types of abuses can include:

- Mental Abuse
- Physical Abuse
- Sexual Abuse
- Alcoholism in the home
- Drug Abuse

Other types of abuses can include:

- Lack of food for meals
- Dirty living conditions
- Violence in the home

Don't allow anyone to threaten you in order to stop you from reporting any kind of abuse.

Call 911 if necessary or contact a social worker immediately for help.

KEEP YOURSELF AND OTHERS SAFE BY SEEKING AND REPORTING ABUSE.

GET HELP AT ANY COST!

Illness

If you are ill, a hospital cannot turn you away. There are also clinics in every city; some work on a sliding scale. If you feel mentally unstable, there are several locations that can help you.

Keep in mind that there are hotlines for suicide prevention. Please reach out if you begin to feel suicidal or suffer from extreme depression. It is not just an emotion; it really is an illness.

If you feel angry and want to hurt yourself or others, please call 911 and get help right away. It is an emergency, and they can send someone to help you. DO NOT HESITATE!

Your Parents' Obligations

Parents have many obligations when it comes to taking care of you. But by law, there are actually very few legal responsibilities parents have to their children, and those end when you turn eighteen.

Parents are required to provide the following; however, they are really not required to give you any more unless they want to.

Basic requirements:

- food
- shelter
- clothing
- basic education
- protect you and keep you safe
- medical attention

Affection is not a requirement. Anything more that you have received from your parents are perks of gratitude, affection, gifts of love for you, all because they love you. You are their child, and they want the best for you.

Some of you have not had responsible parents to show you love and what it feels like to have a real family and affection. This makes it tough because you feel alone. Foster programs do what they can with what they get from the government. For those of you in this position, seek out mentors, not just one or two, but several that you can turn to. They will encourage, support and help you go in the right direction. Fight and work to create the life you want, the life you deserve!

16

Being Homeless

I've never been homeless, and I can bet you haven't either, but I can bet it really sucks! No one chooses to be homeless. If they had a place to go; they would be there. They would have a warm bed, shower, food, and even a job. People are homeless for lots of reasons. Some of the main reasons are mental illness, physical illness, disability, age, and, possibly, the fact that they have been unemployed for so long that no one will give them a chance and they just give up. Some young adults are homeless because they have aged out of some kind of foster care program or have had to leave home due to detrimental circumstances.

At a young age, you won't be homeless for quite a while if you have lots of friends. If you move out and go live with friends, you will be in good shape until their parents get tired of supporting you. After that, out you go. Most young people move from friend's house to friend's house. Most don't want to go back home to hear that dreaded "I told you so" from parents. Others don't get that option.

Your best bet is to take your lecture like the adult you are trying to prove you are—go home and start over in your preparation to move out and be ready. If your parents will not allow this because they are trying to teach you using tough love, what can you do? One choice would be to make a decision about what kind of person you want to be, make that attitude adjustment, humble yourself, and ask your parents one more time but doing it in a very respectful way. Parents want to hear that you have learned your lesson, that you admit error or having made a poor choice. You have nothing to lose. Thank them for listening, and ask them to please reconsider. Most parents want what's best for you and will give you one more chance. That comment is usually followed by a list of new house rules. Suck it up, follow the rules while you *really* get yourself financially ready to make that move.

What If You Become Homeless? What If You Need Help?

Being homeless is not safe for anyone—constant fear, tension with other homeless people, territory wars, law enforcement monitoring, mean people that target and harm homeless people, theft of one another's property, possible physical abuse, and physical fighting. Be assured that you will be no exception to any of these things if you are homeless.

Because once you have run out of roofs to crash under and you are *really* on your own, the time arrives when you have to make some serious tough adult choices.

Nighttime comes every night, and you will need a place to sleep and feel safe or, at least, as safe as you can feel while being homeless. First thing to do is look for homeless shelters. They are typically at churches or community centers that assist the homeless. They have rules that must be followed to be allowed to stay there. The lines to get in are very long and, typically, people sleep on the floor indoors or on cots. Bathrooms are shared by all the people sleeping there that night. If you leave your stuff, you may or may not see it again when you return from the bathroom or anytime that you walk away. If you can't get a bed in a shelter, be prepared to sleep outside somewhere. Select the place carefully, a place where you feel will be safe from other homeless people. These shelters also may provide free meals.

Don't expect anything fancy; the food is donated by people that want to help feed the homeless. The meal will also not be anything like Sunday dinner, more like a simple sandwich or some soup and bread. Fruits and vegetables may be on the menu that night if someone donated any. This is one reason you see people begging for food on the side of the road. Many people drink alcohol, use drugs, use cardboard signs asking for help, and prefer people give them money for booze and drugs. Have you ever seen a sign that says something like "Need money for booze" or "Need money for my next fix"? Of course not because no one would give them a thing.

These are the same people you will see at shelters, under bridges, in parks, and in homeless camps. To get a full experience of being homeless, visit a shelter, pay closer attention to where the homeless gather, go there to experience if this is a community you want to be a part of. This little research of homelessness will give you a *whole new view* of life on the streets. Desperate homeless people will prostitute themselves to be protected, fed, and supplied with drugs and alcohol—a life no young person should *ever* have to experience.

What do you do if you find yourself homeless? As early in the morning as possible, start looking for a shelter because they fill up fast. They may or may not provide meals. If they don't, go to any church and ask if they know where the homeless are fed. In most areas, someone feeds the homeless regularly at the same places. Others may have scheduled dates, locations, and times. *Ask a homeless person. They all know where to get food from all nearby programs.*

If you get sick and need a doctor, you can try going to a clinic. Many cities have free clinics, you just have to find them. You can go to the emergency room. Most emergency rooms can't turn you away if you are really sick.

In preparation for homeless life:

- locate safe sleeping shelters or safe sleeping places;

- locate and know where meals are served to homeless;
- locate and know where clinics and emergency rooms are that serve the homeless;
- locate and know where you can clean up so you don't look homeless. (You look like less of a target for theft and abuse if you are clean and don't look homeless).

If you have lots of stuff and no place to keep it, find a nice big shopping cart to keep your stuff with you. You may also need a tarp if and when the weather gets bad or that you can put down if you have to sleep on the ground.

Do whatever is necessary to never be homeless and on the streets.

17

Human Trafficking

Today more than at any other time in history, the trafficking of young men and women is higher than ever. It is in the news on television and constantly in the online news feeds. Who kidnaps them or convinces them to just walk away with them not knowing they will be kidnapped? What happens to them?

Human traffickers look like everyone around. Some adults, high school and college students are recruited to befriend young future victims, get to know them and earn their trust over a period of time. Depending on the targeted person, it can take hours or days for the person to lure a new "friend" to a set location to be kidnapped and transported to other secret locations. These victims are used in several different ways that are for the sexual and financial benefit of their new owners. Yes, they now own the victim and the victim becomes utilized to earn money for their owners.

The victims are used mostly for the sex trade. Victims may be raped, beaten, drugged, bound, gagged, shackled, handcuffed, or even caged like an animal.

They can and may be used for producing illegal pornographic materials to be sold. These young victims can also be forced into prostitution, can be held captive and sold for sex in brothel style locations to be transported to any place in the world. Victims, mostly women may be sold to someone who will hold them captive for their own pleasures.

Victims are sometimes threatened, drugged, cleaned and dressed for photographs to be taken and used to market and sell the person. They are sold on secret auctions or by word of mouth to the highest bidder.

Human traffickers are in this business to make money using people against their will.

Research how to be safe from human trafficking, but mostly, use common sense and go with your gut instinct.

Young women are more likely to be victimized, abused, kidnapped, sold and prostituted than young men because their sex and a trafficker's ability for higher financial benefits. Keep in mind that young men are also a commodity. Take all precautionary measures to be safe and not become a statistic of human trafficking.

WORKBOOK SECTION

Getting Ready to Move Out

- Employment Guide
- Information Preparation
- Log Pages

Move-out Time Frame: One Year Before You Move Out (A Little Chat Before You Get Started)

1. Social Media
2. Preparing for an Interview
3. Interview Possible Sample Questions (Employer and Employee)
4. Presenting Yourself to the Interviewer
5. Log Sheets

    Employment

    Banking

    Credit Building

    House Hunting

Move-out Time Frame: One Year Before You Move Out

If you plan to move out next year, this year is when you would be starting to get yourself ready. Organization will be the key to a successful and amicable move. Moving out is *huge*! It's one of the truest adult things a young adult will do. But it isn't just that. It's showing yourself, your parents, and those around you that you are mature enough to do this and succeed!

Once you turn eighteen, life is not all yours if you live at home. Parents' house, parents' rules. If you are eighteen and live in your own place, your house, your rules. It's all about you when you make it out of mom and dad's and can afford to live on your own without their money.

Some parents tell their kids that once they move out, there is no coming back. Some parents mean it, some parents don't, and some parents change their minds. All parents are different. Most parents love their children.

Be open with your family. Talk about your plans, your goals, and your dreams; and work hard to reach them. Let your parents or guardians know what your goals and plans are for the coming year. They can help by giving you guidance and advice. They will point you in the right direction. Your parents or guardians will be the ones to support and guide you as you start planning one of the biggest days of your life. Young adults who age out of foster or government care programs don't get the opportunity to "Go Home." They have to make it. They don't have a choice. If you are one of these young adults, my best advice is keep helping yourself and asking for help.

Seek out a mentor that you respect and who is willing to guide and help you succeed. Don't give up. You may have more than one mentor in your life, and that is even better!

This workbook will get you started and help you get organized.

1

Social Media

Now that you are beginning your adult life and are going to be out there looking for a job and a place to live, this is something you need to be *very* aware of.

Your social media life has a direct arrow pointing at the reflection of who you really are. Employers are now looking at social media before even offering an interview. They don't want to waste their time interviewing someone that does not fit their business personality.

What you post on your Facebook, Twitter, MySpace, or any other social media account may be seen by potential employers, helping them make an assessment of you before they even meet you or helping them decide if you will even take a step inside their doors.

Young adults love posting their parties, jokes, and comments and sharing photos that may be funny and amusing to their peers but, maybe, not so much to future or potential employers. That alone may take you right out of the job you apply for. So start cleaning up your social media posts or making all your social media accounts as invisible as possible. You may think "I should be able to do whatever I want on my time." This should, in fact, be the case, but in the grown-up world, it really isn't like that at all.

Jobs today are at will. This means that they don't have to have a reason to hire you or fire you.

Please be careful that your online social media life doesn't ruin your real life.

What you post is what you boast.

2

Preparing for an Interview

Before going on any interview, look up the company. Learn about it and what its business mission is. Regardless of how menial it may seem, employers are impressed with the fact that you took time to learn about their business and its details.

Look at the announcement for the position that you are applying for, and be familiar with what you will say that best describes why you would be the best person for the job.

Look up cover letter samples that you can use as guides to prepare a cover letter, specifically in the name of that interviewer if you know their name, or to the hiring manager if you don't know who will be interviewing you.

Cover letter should only be a couple of short paragraphs.

Look up sample resumés that you can use as guides and prepare a resumé. (When preparing cover letters, personalize your cover letter to the person you are being interviewed by. Update this every time you have a different interview). Before making copies, have someone look over your cover letter and resumé to check for errors. Once completed, print out two to four copies of your cover letter and resumé. You will want to hand one of each to the interviewer so you can follow along with your own copy in hand. Present your cover letter on top of your resumé.

Prepare and print a list of questions you have for the interviewer. You will want to be able to look at your list in case some of the questions were not answered.

Arrive ten minutes early for your interview. Leave your cell phone in the car or turn it off. *Do not* put it on vibrate because it may still make noise during the interview.

Below you will find some questions you can ask. Feel free to add any of your own questions or leave out any that will not apply. Place your cover letter, resumé, and list of questions in an easy-to-access case or folder. (Do not take your papers in a backpack).

Be prepared to tell the interviewer a little bit about yourself, at some point, during your interview. Look the interviewer in the eye and share main points about yourself. Sell yourself as if you were your favorite product.

Men and Women

When you get an interview

Research the company as soon as you have the interview set up. If you know about the company, you can use some of the information in your personalized cover letter. Know the company history, founder, when the company was started, what they do. Learn things about the company that you can share when a question comes up like "What do you know about our company?" and that question will come up most of the time. Because all jobs are different and all employers are different, you always want to dress professionally for the interview. It doesn't matter if you have seen the employees of that company wearing jeans and T-shirts to work, it is never okay to wear jeans and T-shirts to any job interview.

Now that I have that out of the way, the first impression you make is the most important. How well you are groomed makes a very big difference and so does how neat, clean, and pressed your clothes are.

Men

A few days before the interview:

1. In a nice folder or carry case, put together your cover letter and resumé. (Don't ever take a backpack as a briefcase to an interview).
2. Practice the interview with someone. Go over it a few times until you are comfortable with the answers and potential employer questions.

Day before the interview:

1. Call to confirm your interview appointment.
2. Go to the location of your interview so you know exactly where you are going. If you don't and wait for the day of your interview and you rely on your cell phone map or ask Siri (sometimes Siri is in a totally different place), chances are you are going to be late. Be smart, go to the location, and be sure exactly where you are going. This will also give you peace of mind.
3. Select your interview clothes; make sure they are clean and pressed. If you have sleeve body art, wear a long-sleeved shirt. Tie is optional unless your research points to a higher standard of dressing. Wear slacks, not jeans, shorts, or any casual clothing. Interviews require a semiformal attire. Select a suit, dress slacks or khakis, and a neat and clean

pair of shoes. If tucking in a shirt, select a belt that matches your shoes—makes you look really crisp!

Day of the interview:

Start your morning with a nice refreshing shower that will help you relax and feel better. Apply your deodorant. (People who are nervous tend to sweat more).

1. If you have facial or other visible piercing, best advice is that you remove it for the interview and ask about it during the interview. The interviewer will advise you on the company policy regarding body art and piercing.
2. Hair should be clean and neatly combed. Men with longer hair should keep in mind that pulling hair back gives you a cleaner, more professional, and approachable look.
3. Make sure you are clean-shaven, or if you have facial hair, it is trimmed in a neat and clean way. (You don't want your facial hair to make you look unkempt).
4. Don't wear sneakers, old or worn-out shoes. Select a nice pair of neat and clean shoes. If you don't have any, ask your parents if they can help you get a pair. You can also get some at a low-priced shoe store or a gently used clothing secondhand store. They are usually very reasonably priced. Try to wear a matching belt too.
5. Before heading out the door, be sure to brush your teeth.

Ladies

A few days before the interview:

1. In a nice folder or carry case, put together your cover letter and resumé. (Don't ever take a backpack as a briefcase to an interview).
2. Practice the interview with someone. Go over it a few times until you are comfortable with the answers and potential employer questions.

A day before the interview:

1. Call to confirm your interview appointment
2. Go to the location of your interview so you know exactly where you are going. If you don't and wait for the day of your interview and you rely on your cell phone map or ask Siri (sometimes Siri is in a totally different place), chances are you are going to be late. Be smart, go to the location, and be sure exactly where you are going. This will also give you peace of mind.
3. Select your interview clothes; make sure they are clean and pressed. If you have sleeve body art, wear a long-sleeved blouse or suit jacket. If you don't have body art on your arms, select a blouse or suit that fits the climate. Ladies, select conservative clothing—no plunging necklines, no blouses that show lots of cleavage, nothing see-though, or provocative. Select daytime makeup styles that look more professional. If you are wearing jewelry, don't wear anything inappropriate, like giant hoops or big bright colors. Select something toned down and conservative. Shoes should be neat, clean, and reasonable—no three-inch heals, strapless shoes, flip-flops or shoes that appear to be unprofessional. A rule of thumb, if there is a fire, can you run out of the building in those shoes and not kill yourself or block others from getting to safety?

Day of the interview:

Start your morning with a nice refreshing shower that will help you relax and feel better. Apply your deodorant. (People who are nervous tend to sweat more).

1. If you have visible piercing, best advice is that you remove it for the interview and ask about it during the interview. The interviewer will advise you on the company policy regarding body art and piercing.

2. Makeup should be applied in a manner that is conservative. No wild or super bright colors.
3. Hair should be clean and neatly combed, or styled hair should be away from your eyes. A professional and conservative hairstyle is usually preferred.
4. Don't wear sneakers, flip-flops, and old or worn-out shoes. Select a nice pair of neat and clean shoes. If you don't have any, ask your parents if they can help you get a pair. You can also get some at a low-priced shoe store or a gently used clothing secondhand store. They are usually very reasonably priced.
5. Before heading out the door, be sure to brush your teeth.

Job Insight

There may be other questions directly related to the position you are applying for. That's why you should research the company and find out how you can make yourself the *best* choice. Sell yourself through your leisure activities, school activities, personal experiences, and how they all mesh into the experience they are looking for.

Are you applying at a fast-food place or restaurant? If you like to cook, grill barbecue, help in the kitchen, or just enjoy cooking, use that as a selling point.

Are you applying for a data-entry or computer-related position? If you are proficient on your computer, specify the programs you use most and programs that can be associated with that position. Let the interviewer know what programs you are familiar with. Let the interviewer know specifically what programs they are and how they relate to the position you are applying for.

You get the picture?

3

Interviewer Possible Sample Questions

How will you answer them? (Fill in the blanks.)

Is this your first job interview? *If you say no, they will ask where else you have applied. If you were previously employed or are currently working, they may ask if they can contact those employers for a reference. Be prepared for this. If you do have another job and your employer doesn't know you are looking to change jobs, you can say no and that you plan on giving proper notice once you have another job lined up. If your current employer knows you are looking for another job and doesn't mind giving you a reference, you can tell the interviewer that it's fine for them to call your current employer.

How many other companies are you applying at? ________________
Where are you applying for jobs? ________________________

____

____

What do you know about our company? ____________________

____

____

Why do you want to work for this company? ________________

____

____

Did someone refer you to our company? ________Who? ________
Do you think you are responsible enough to fulfill a work schedule?
____

Do you intend on continuing your education if you are hired? _____
How will you keep up with school and a job? ________________
____
____

What do you plan on studying in the future? ________________
____
____

What are your hobbies? ____________________________
____
____

What do you do for fun? ___________________________
____
____

Do you participate in any community or volunteer activities? _____
If so, what are they: ____________________________
____

Are you looking for full-time or part-time work? ____________
If you are hired, can you work nights and weekends? ___________
If you are hired, can you work on holidays? ________________
If hired, how will you get to and from work? _______________
Where do you see yourself in five years? (They always ask this question)! ____________________________
____
____
____
____

Where do you live and with whom? (Or they ask, do you live nearby)?
____
____

Tell me a little bit about yourself. *This question is when you sell yourself as if you are your favorite product!*

Potential Questions You Can Ask

Questions *you* may ask an employer during your interview:

Is this a full-time or part-time position? (unless stated in the job description)
Is there training involved? (unless stated in the job description)
Is there a probationary period? If so, how long is it?
What are the work hours?
Are the workdays flexible?
Does the company have paid holidays?
Does the company offer paid sick days?
What is the salary range for this position? (unless stated in the job description)
What benefits come with the position? (i.e., vacation, medical, dental, 401(k))
If benefits are offered, when are they effective?
Is this a company I can grow with?
How soon will you make a decision and fill the position?
Is there anything else I need to know?

These questions may be asked by you if they are not answered during your interview.

Now you are ready to head out the door for your interview.

Leave home early so you will not be late. Try to be there about ten minutes before your scheduled interview time.

Once you arrive, check in with the person at the desk, door, counter, or office window.
Politely tell them your full name, why you are there, and who you are there to see. For example, your introduction to the person receiving you: "Good afternoon (or morning, depending on time of day). I'm Jamie Jobseeker. I have an appointment for an interview with The Hiring Manager at 1:30 today."

Once you have checked in, you may be asked to take a seat and wait, or you will be escorted to the interview office or room. Do not be on your cell phone while you are waiting to be interviewed. Make sure your cell phone is off or preferably in your car.

Try to relax even though you may be a little stressed out.

4

Presenting Yourself to the Interviewer

If you are escorted into an office or room and the interviewer is present, introduce yourself as you shake hands. Have a firm handshake, but don't make the interviewer say uncle. Look the interviewer in the eye and show self-confidence.

If the interviewer asks you to take a seat, do so, and take out a copy of your cover letter and resumé. Hand them to the interviewer with the cover letter on top. You can say this is your first job interview and that you are a little nervous. They understand; they were once in your seat too.

Don't fidget or be looking around the room. Focus on the interviewer, keep your eyes on that person, and listen attentively.

When the interviewer is explaining the company and position, he or she may stop to ask if you have any questions about what was just explained. If you don't understand, ask questions. Do not assume.

Take a quick glance at your questions sheet and ask any questions that were not answered that you still want to ask.

The End of the Interview

Once the interview is over and you both stand up, *as you are shaking hands*, you may want to say something like, "Thank you for your time. I appreciate the opportunity to have an interview with you about this position. I hope you will seriously consider me for the job. I promise to give my best effort if I am selected."

You can do this!

* Super helpful hint: send a thank you card.

Practice writing your thank you card:

Dear ____

____

____

____

____

Sign your name here

5

Tracking Log Sheets

Employment

Banking

Credit Building

House Hunting

Make copies of any tracking logs sheets needed.

Employment Tracking Log

Application log for this company:

Company name ___________________________________
Address ____________________ City ______ State ______ Zip ___
Position you are going to apply for ______________________
Name of hiring manager ____________________________
Telephone number of hiring manager ___________________
Email address of hiring manager ______________________

Date you applied ___________ Did you get the interview? _________
Who will be interviewing you? ___________________________
When and what time is your interview? ______________________
Did you prepare yourself by using the section "How to Prepare for an Interview"? ______________________________
Did you arrive on time, a few minutes early, or were you late? _____
____

If you were late, what could you have done differently to have made it to the interview on time?

____

____

What questions didn't you know the answers to?

____

____

What questions did you forget to ask?

____

____

What did you like about the interview?

____

____

What didn't you like about the interview?

____

____

What will you do differently in the next interview?

____

____

Did you mail a thank you card? ____ When did you send it? ______
When will you call back to check on your application status? ______
What's the status of your application? ____________________

Application log for this company:

Company name ____________________
Address ____________ City ______ State ______ Zip ___
Position you are going to apply for ____________________
Name of hiring manager ____________________
Telephone number of hiring manager ____________________
Email address of hiring manager ____________________

Date you applied __________ Did you get the interview? ______
Who will be interviewing you? ____________________
When and what time is your interview? ____________________
Did you prepare yourself by using the section "How to Prepare for an Interview"? ____________________
Did you arrive on time, a few minutes early, or were you late? ____

____

If you were late, what could you have done differently to have made it to the interview on time?

____

____

What questions didn't you know the answers to?

____

____

What questions did you forget to ask?

____

____

What did you like about the interview?

____

____

What didn't you like about the interview?

____

____

What will you do differently in the next interview?

____

____

Did you mail a thank you card? ____ When did you send it? _______
When will you call back to check on your application status? _______
What's the status of your application? ____________________

Application log for this company:

Company name ______________________________
Address __________________ City ______ State ______ Zip ___
Position you are going to apply for ____________________
Name of hiring manager ________________________
Telephone number of hiring manager ___________________
Email address of hiring manager _____________________

Date you applied __________ Did you get the interview? _________
Who will be interviewing you? ________________________
When and what time is your interview? ____________________
Did you prepare yourself by using the section "How to Prepare for an Interview"? ______________________________
Did you arrive on time, a few minutes early, or were you late? _____

____

If you were late, what could you have done differently to have made it to the interview on time?

____

____

What questions didn't you know the answers to?

____

____

What questions did you forget to ask?

____

____

What did you like about the interview?

____

____

What didn't you like about the interview?

____

____

What will you do differently in the next interview?

____

____

Did you mail a thank you card? ____ When did you send it? _______
When will you call back to check on your application status? _______
What's the status of your application? ______________________

Application log for this company:

Company name ____________________________________
Address _________________ City ______ State ______ Zip ___
Position you are going to apply for _______________________
Name of hiring manager ______________________________
Telephone number of hiring manager _____________________
Email address of hiring manager _________________________

Date you applied ___________ Did you get the interview? _________
Who will be interviewing you? ____________________________
When and what time is your interview? ______________________
Did you prepare yourself by using the section "How to Prepare for an Interview"? ______________________________________
Did you arrive on time, a few minutes early, or were you late? ______

____

If you were late, what could you have done differently to have made it to the interview on time?

____

____

What questions didn't you know the answers to?

____

____

What questions did you forget to ask?

____

____

What did you like about the interview?

____

____

What didn't you like about the interview?

____

____

What will you do differently in the next interview?

____

____

Did you mail a thank you card? ____ When did you send it? _______
When will you call back to check on your application status? _______
What's the status of your application? ____________________

Application log for this company:

Company name ______________________________
Address __________________ City _____ State _____ Zip ___
Position you are going to apply for ____________________
Name of hiring manager ____________________________
Telephone number of hiring manager ____________________
Email address of hiring manager ______________________

Date you applied __________ Did you get the interview? _________
Who will be interviewing you? __________________________
When and what time is your interview? _____________________
Did you prepare yourself by using the section "How to Prepare for an Interview"? ______________________________
Did you arrive on time, a few minutes early, or were you late? _____

____

If you were late, what could you have done differently to have made it to the interview on time?

____

____

What questions didn't you know the answers to?

____

____

What questions did you forget to ask?

____

____

What did you like about the interview?

____

____

What didn't you like about the interview?

____

____

What will you do differently in the next interview?

____

____

Did you mail a thank you card? ____ When did you send it? _______
When will you call back to check on your application status? _______
What's the status of your application? ______________________

Application log for this company:

Company name ______________________________
Address ________________ City ______ State ______ Zip ___
Position you are going to apply for ____________________
Name of hiring manager ____________________________
Telephone number of hiring manager __________________
Email address of hiring manager _____________________

Date you applied __________ Did you get the interview? _________
Who will be interviewing you? ________________________
When and what time is your interview? ___________________
Did you prepare yourself by using the section "How to Prepare for an Interview"? ________________________________
Did you arrive on time, a few minutes early, or were you late? _____

____

If you were late, what could you have done differently to have made it to the interview on time?

___

___

What questions didn't you know the answers to?

___

___

What questions did you forget to ask?

___

___

What did you like about the interview?

___

___

What didn't you like about the interview?

___

___

What will you do differently in the next interview?

___

___

Did you mail a thank you card? ____ When did you send it? ______
When will you call back to check on your application status? ______
What's the status of your application? ______

Application log for this company:

Company name ______
Address ______ City ______ State ______ Zip ___
Position you are going to apply for ______
Name of hiring manager ______
Telephone number of hiring manager ______
Email address of hiring manager ______

Date you applied ______ Did you get the interview? ______
Who will be interviewing you? ______
When and what time is your interview? ______

Did you prepare yourself by using the section "How to Prepare for an Interview"? ______________________________

Did you arrive on time, a few minutes early, or were you late? _____

____

If you were late, what could you have done differently to have made it to the interview on time?

____

____

What questions didn't you know the answers to?

____

____

What questions did you forget to ask?

____

____

What did you like about the interview?

____

____

What didn't you like about the interview?

____

____

What will you do differently in the next interview?

____

____

Did you mail a thank you card? ____ When did you send it? _______

When will you call back to check on your application status? _______

What's the status of your application? ______________________

Application log for this company:

Company name ______________________________

Address ____________________ City ______ State ______ Zip ___

Position you are going to apply for ______________________

Name of hiring manager ______________________________

Telephone number of hiring manager ______________________

Email address of hiring manager ______________________

Date you applied ___________ Did you get the interview? _________
Who will be interviewing you? ______________________________
When and what time is your interview? _________________________
Did you prepare yourself by using the section "How to Prepare for an Interview"? ____
Did you arrive on time, a few minutes early, or were you late? _____
____

If you were late, what could you have done differently to have made it to the interview on time?

____

____

What questions didn't you know the answers to?

____

____

What questions did you forget to ask?

____

____

What did you like about the interview?

____

____

What didn't you like about the interview?

____

____

What will you do differently in the next interview?

____

____

Did you mail a thank you card? ____ When did you send it? _______
When will you call back to check on your application status? _______
What's the status of your application? ____________________

Application log for this company:

Company name ______________________________________
Address ____________________ City ______ State ______ Zip ___
Position you are going to apply for __________________________
Name of hiring manager _____________________________

Telephone number of hiring manager ____________________
Email address of hiring manager ____________________

Date you applied __________ Did you get the interview? __________
Who will be interviewing you? ____________________
When and what time is your interview? ____________________
Did you prepare yourself by using the section "How to Prepare for an Interview"? ____________________
Did you arrive on time, a few minutes early, or were you late? _____
____

If you were late, what could you have done differently to have made it to the interview on time?

____

____

What questions didn't you know the answers to?

____

____

What questions did you forget to ask?

____

____

What did you like about the interview?

____

____

What didn't you like about the interview?

____

____

What will you do differently in the next interview?

____

____

Did you mail a thank you card? ____ When did you send it? _______
When will you call back to check on your application status? _______
What's the status of your application? ____________________

Application log for this company:

Company name ______________________________
Address ____________ City ______ State ______ Zip ___
Position you are going to apply for ______________________
Name of hiring manager ______________________________
Telephone number of hiring manager __________________
Email address of hiring manager ____________________

Date you applied __________ Did you get the interview? _________
Who will be interviewing you? ___________________________
When and what time is your interview? ______________________
Did you prepare yourself by using the section "How to Prepare for an Interview"? ______________________________
Did you arrive on time, a few minutes early, or were you late? _____
____

If you were late, what could you have done differently to have made it to the interview on time?

____
____

What questions didn't you know the answers to?

____
____

What questions did you forget to ask?

____
____

What did you like about the interview?

____
____

What didn't you like about the interview?

____
____

What will you do differently in the next interview?

____
____

Did you mail a thank you card? ____ When did you send it? ________
When will you call back to check on your application status? ________
What's the status of your application? ______________________________

Banking

List banks and credit unions you researched. *Look into a minimum of three banks and two credit unions

How did you research this bank/credit union?
___ Online ___ In person ___ By phone
Name of bank ___________________________
Contact phone number ___________ Email address ___________
What do I need to open a checking and savings account? ________
____
Is there a minimum amount to open an account? ___________
Is a minimum balance required? ________ If so, how much? _____
Is there a monthly fee to have a checking account? ___________
If so, what is the fee? ___________________________
Do checks get issued? _________ Who pays for the checks? _____
How are they paid for? _________ How much do they cost? ______
Do you accept direct deposit from an employer? _____________
Do you provide online banking? ___________________
Do you offer overdraft protection? _________________
Is there a fee for returned checks if there is not enough money in the account to pay a check? ___________________
If so, how much is the returned check fee? _______________
Do you offer an ATM card for the account, and is there a fee to use it? ___________________________
If so, what is the fee to use the ATM card? ______________
Can the ATM card be used at other banks? _______________
If so, what is the fee? ___________________________
When the ATM card is used at stores, online, or at gas stations, is there a fee? ___________________________
If so, what is the fee? ________ How and when are fees charged? ___

What other benefits are there to bank with you? ______________
____
____

Notes: ____
____
____
____
____

How did you research this bank/credit union?
___ Online ___ In person ___ By phone
Name of bank ____
Contact phone number __________ Email address __________
What do I need to open a checking and savings account? __________
____
Is there a minimum amount to open an account? __________
Is a minimum balance required? ________ If so, how much? _____
Is there a monthly fee to have a checking account? __________
If so, what is the fee? ____________________________________
Do checks get issued? _________ Who pays for the checks? _____
How are they paid for? _________ How much do they cost? ______
Do you accept direct deposit from an employer? __________
Do you provide online banking? __________
Do you offer overdraft protection? __________
Is there a fee for returned checks if there is not enough money in the account to pay a check? __________
If so, how much is the returned check fee? __________
Do you offer an ATM card for the account, and is there a fee to use it? ____________________________________
If so, what is the fee to use the ATM card? __________
Can the ATM card be used at other banks? __________
If so, what is the fee? ____________________________________
When the ATM card is used at stores, online, or at gas stations, is there a fee? ____________________________________
If so, what is the fee? ________ How and when are fees charged? ___

What other benefits are there to bank with you? __________
____
____

Notes: ____
____
____
____
____

How did you research this bank/credit union?
___ Online ___ In person ___ By phone
Name of bank ______________________________________
Contact phone number ___________ Email address ____________
What do I need to open a checking and savings account? _________
____
Is there a minimum amount to open an account? _____________
Is a minimum balance required? ________ If so, how much? _____
Is there a monthly fee to have a checking account? ____________
If so, what is the fee? ______________________________
Do checks get issued? _________ Who pays for the checks? ______
How are they paid for? _________ How much do they cost? _______
Do you accept direct deposit from an employer? ______________
Do you provide online banking? ________________________
Do you offer overdraft protection? ______________________
Is there a fee for returned checks if there is not enough money in the account to pay a check? ______________________________
If so, how much is the returned check fee? _________________
Do you offer an ATM card for the account, and is there a fee to use it? ____
If so, what is the fee to use the ATM card? _________________
Can the ATM card be used at other banks? _________________
If so, what is the fee? ______________________________
When the ATM card is used at stores, online, or at gas stations, is there a fee? ______________________________________
If so, what is the fee? ________ How and when are fees charged? ___

What other benefits are there to bank with you? ______________
____
____

Notes: ____

____

____

____

____

How did you research this bank/credit union?
___ Online ___ In person ___ By phone
Name of bank ____
Contact phone number ____________ Email address ____________
What do I need to open a checking and savings account? __________

____

Is there a minimum amount to open an account? ______________
Is a minimum balance required? ________ If so, how much? _____
Is there a monthly fee to have a checking account? ____________
If so, what is the fee? _________________________________
Do checks get issued? _________ Who pays for the checks? ______
How are they paid for? _________ How much do they cost? _______
Do you accept direct deposit from an employer? ______________
Do you provide online banking? __________________________
Do you offer overdraft protection? ________________________
Is there a fee for returned checks if there is not enough money in the account to pay a check? __________________________________
If so, how much is the returned check fee? ___________________
Do you offer an ATM card for the account, and is there a fee to use it? ____
If so, what is the fee to use the ATM card? __________________
Can the ATM card be used at other banks? ___________________
If so, what is the fee? _________________________________
When the ATM card is used at stores, online, or at gas stations, is there a fee? ____
If so, what is the fee? ________ How and when are fees charged? ___

What other benefits are there to bank with you? _______________

____

____

Notes: ____
____
____
____
____

How did you research this bank/credit union?
___ Online ___ In person ___ By phone
Name of bank ____________________________________
Contact phone number ____________ Email address ____________
What do I need to open a checking and savings account? _________
____
Is there a minimum amount to open an account? ____________
Is a minimum balance required? ________ If so, how much? _____
Is there a monthly fee to have a checking account? ____________
If so, what is the fee? _____________________________
Do checks get issued? _________ Who pays for the checks? ______
How are they paid for? _________ How much do they cost? _______
Do you accept direct deposit from an employer? _______________
Do you provide online banking? _________________________
Do you offer overdraft protection? ______________________
Is there a fee for returned checks if there is not enough money in the account to pay a check? ___________________________
If so, how much is the returned check fee? _________________
Do you offer an ATM card for the account, and is there a fee to use it? ____
If so, what is the fee to use the ATM card? _________________
Can the ATM card be used at other banks? _________________
If so, what is the fee? _____________________________
When the ATM card is used at stores, online, or at gas stations, is there a fee? ____________________________________
If so, what is the fee? ________ How and when are fees charged? ___

What other benefits are there to bank with you? ____________
____
____

Notes: ____
____
____
____
____

How did you research this bank/credit union?
___ Online ___ In person ___ By phone
Name of bank ____
Contact phone number ___________ Email address ____________
What do I need to open a checking and savings account? _________
____
Is there a minimum amount to open an account? ______________
Is a minimum balance required? ________ If so, how much? _____
Is there a monthly fee to have a checking account? ____________
If so, what is the fee? _________________________________
Do checks get issued? _________ Who pays for the checks? ______
How are they paid for? _________ How much do they cost? _______
Do you accept direct deposit from an employer? _______________
Do you provide online banking? __________________________
Do you offer overdraft protection? ________________________
Is there a fee for returned checks if there is not enough money in the account to pay a check? ___________________________________
If so, how much is the returned check fee? ____________________
Do you offer an ATM card for the account, and is there a fee to use it? ____
If so, what is the fee to use the ATM card? __________________
Can the ATM card be used at other banks? ____________________
If so, what is the fee? _________________________________
When the ATM card is used at stores, online, or at gas stations, is there a fee? ______________________________________
If so, what is the fee? ________ How and when are fees charged? ___

What other benefits are there to bank with you? _______________
____
____

Notes: ____

____

____

____

____

Credit Building

Review the section about credit scores in the beginning of your book to better understand your credit because establishing credit once you have a job is very important for your future. Typically, a minimum of three to four accounts are required if you are applying for a loan. How long you have had the accounts is one of the things considered by banks and others offering you loans. The available balances don't have to be high. The payment history just has to show that you pay your bills on time. One of the secrets to great credit is to always only carry 20–25 percent or less of the amount you are eligible for and to add a few extra dollars to each payment, not just to pay the minimum due.

Credit reports include more information than just credit data. For example, they show personal data like your address, birthday, and your employer.

Student credit cards are available. If you're a student, try a credit card specifically tailored for students. Student credit cards are meant for younger people who usually don't qualify for higher-level credit cards. However, there are some that offer cash back or other rewards when you use them. Take a look at the Discover It for Students or Journey Student Rewards credit card on the Capital One banking website.

Another way to establish credit is with a secured credit card. Since you may have no credit score on file, consider a secured credit card, which almost always guarantees you will be approved for a credit card. A secured credit card requires a cash deposit; that is what your credit limit will be on your new secured credit card. The deposit usually can be from $300 to $1,000. These kinds of cards are good if you're just starting out and have little or no credit. By having this money in a savings account, you are a low risk to the bank giving you the card. Most banks and credit unions offer secured credit cards. Without a secured credit card and being a new consumer, you may have to pay higher interest rates until you prove you are a good loan risk. You can establish credit several different ways. Start slowly. Don't apply to several different places at once. A secured card should be your first choice. If that doesn't go well, apply at a department or electronics store. Chances are, you may be approved for as little as $200 just to get you started, and see how you handle your payments and what your spending habits will be.

Credit Log

List of companies I have applied for credit with:

Date applied for credit ________________ Amount requested ________
Name of company ____
Accepted ____________________________ Denied ________________

Date applied for credit ________________ Amount requested ________
Name of company ____
Accepted ____________________________ Denied ________________

Date applied for credit ________________ Amount requested ________
Name of company ____
Accepted ____________________________ Denied ________________

Date applied for credit ________________ Amount requested ________
Name of company ____
Accepted ____________________________ Denied ________________

Date applied for credit ________________ Amount requested ________
Name of company ____
Accepted ____________________________ Denied ________________

Date applied for credit ________________ Amount requested ________
Name of company ____
Accepted ____________________________ Denied ________________

House Hunting Tracking Log

Hopefully, by now, you have read the section about looking for a new place to live.

House hunting is time-consuming. I recommend you make lots of calls before driving all over the place. Younger renters tend to get rejected more often because of their age and the reputation that most are just learning the ropes, and many landlords look at younger potential tenants as, possibly, irresponsible kids they will have to deal with.

Make it a point to sell yourself by phone first. It's a good idea for you have personal character references in writing to present to potential landlords. Ask teachers, professors, neighbors, employers, and adult friends who are in good standing in the community for written references, and ask if it's okay that a potential landlord calls to ask questions about you and what kind of person you are.

Once you have your reference letters in hand, make several copies and keep the original in case you need to make more copies.

Keep a list of places you call, and schedule appointments to go see what they have to offer you as a rental. Ask the questions outlined in the house section so you are ready, and know what it will cost you to live at any place you visit.

Dress appropriately, use good manners, say please and thank you. This really helps too!

House Hunting Log

Date of application: ______________________________

Name of place applied: ______________________________

Address: ______________________________

Landlord's name: ______________________________

Phone number: ______________ Email: ______________

Date to follow-up with landlord: ______________________________

What you liked about the place:

____

____

Landlord comments:

____

____

____

Date of application: ______________________________

Name of place applied: ______________________________

Address: ______________________________

Landlord's name: ______________________________

Phone number: ______________ Email: ______________

Date to follow-up with landlord: ______________________________

What you liked about the place:

____

____

Landlord comments:

____

____

____

Date of application: ______________________________

Name of place applied: ______________________________

Address: ______________________________

Landlord's name: ______________________________

Phone number: ______________ Email: ______________

Date to follow-up with landlord: ______________________________

What you liked about the place:

____

____

Landlord comments:

____

____

____

Date of application: ______________________________

Name of place applied: ____________________________

Address: ____

Landlord's name: ________________________________

Phone number: _______________ Email: _______________

Date to follow-up with landlord: ______________________

What you liked about the place:

____

____

Landlord comments:

____

____

____

Date of application: ______________________________

Name of place applied: ____________________________

Address: ____

Landlord's name: ________________________________

Phone number: _______________ Email: _______________

Date to follow-up with landlord: ______________________

What you liked about the place:

____

____

Landlord comments:

____

____

____

Date of application: ______________________________

Name of place applied: ______________________________

Address: ______________________________

Landlord's name: ______________________________

Phone number: ______________ Email: ______________

Date to follow-up with landlord: ______________________________

What you liked about the place:

____

____

Landlord comments:

____

____

____

Date of application: ______________________________

Name of place applied: ______________________________

Address: ______________________________

Landlord's name: ______________________________

Phone number: ______________ Email: ______________

Date to follow-up with landlord: ______________________________

What you liked about the place:

____

____

Landlord comments:

____

____

____

Date of application: ______________________________

Name of place applied: ______________________________

Address: ______________________________

Landlord's name: ______________________________

Phone number: ______________ Email: ______________

Date to follow-up with landlord: ______________________________

What you liked about the place:

____

____

Landlord comments:

____

____

____

Summary

You have taken the first step in obtaining some of the most important information you need to start preparing for life on your own. You're ready to start taking these steps one at a time. You're armed with the proper tools to set yourself up to look for and interview to get a job, open bank accounts, establish credit, seek housing, save up deposits for a new home and utilities, accumulate household goods, and look for other options that may be available to you. You have insight on life game changers, being homeless, date rape, human trafficking, drug use, and getting medical attention.

If you are in a foster program now, you know where to look for and find resources specifically for you; selecting mentors is a key to success, and no one has to go through life alone.

This is the guide that will fill you in on the things that may not be learned in most homes, schools, communities, and colleges.

Never be too afraid or have too much pride to ask for help. Failure only comes from not trying.

You can do it! This is your map.

About the Author

Ashley Anello is a resident of San Marcos, California. She was born in San Diego and due to very personal circumstances left home at the age of seventeen, leaving high school before graduation. By the time she was eighteen, she had the self-motivation to go on and receive her high school diploma. She continued her education and currently holds two college degrees, in addition to being educated to practice Clinical Hypnotherapy and Bio-Energy therapy.

Ashley is the very proud mother of two adult children and two beautiful granddaughters. Ashley is also a proud military veteran having served in a combination of active duty and as a military reservist in the U.S. Army.

She is currently a full time "Pack & Go" Realtor in San Diego County, a member of the Rotary Club and is associated with several organizations that assist children, young adults, veterans and others in need. She is an advocate for higher education, self-determination and is willing to help anyone who is trying to help themselves.

CPSIA information can be obtained
at www.ICGtesting.com
Printed in the USA
FSHW01n0900090618
49038FS

9 781642 981919